NATURE-FRIENDLY ORDINANCES:
LOCAL MEASURES TO CONSERVE BIODIVERSITY

by James M. McElfish Jr.

D1518440

ENVIRONMENTAL LAW INSTITUTE
WASHINGTON, D.C.

Acknowledgments

The author thanks the Doris Duke Charitable Foundation for its support of this work by the Environmental Law Institute's (ELI's) Sustainable Use of Land and State Biodiversity Programs. ELI is a member of the foundation's Consortium on Biodiversity and Land Use, together with Defenders of Wildlife, Island Press, and NatureServe. ELI staff contributing to this book included then-Staff Attorney Pooja Parikh, who worked on the descriptions of the land use regulatory tools and the ecological guidelines; Research Associate Elizabeth Seeger, who researched and wrote most of the community profiles; and former legal intern Chris Saporita, who researched and wrote about proffers, transfer of development rights, and purchase of development rights. Additional thanks to Chris Duerksen, Richard Haeuber, Lori Hidinger, Bill Klein, John Nolon, Laura Hood Watchman, and to my ELI colleague and partner in biodiversity conservation Jessica Wilkinson for their wise guidance and advice.

About the Author

J ames M. McElfish Jr. is a Senior Attorney at the Environmental Law Institute (ELI), where he directs the Institute's Sustainable Use of Land Program. His publications include, among others, *State Environmental Law* in THE LAW OF ENVIRONMENTAL PROTECTION (Clark, Boardman, Callaghan 1987 updated annually), the book THE ENVIRONMENTAL REGULATION OF COAL MINING (Envtl. L. Inst. 1989), *Learning From the Past and Looking to the Future* in JOHN NOLON, NEW GROUND: THE ADVENT OF LOCAL ENVIRONMENTAL LAW (Envtl. L. Inst. 2003), and approximately 50 ELI research reports and scholarly articles. McElfish served on the American Planning Association's Directorate for its *Growing Smarter*^{TM} *Legislative Guidebook*. He is a 1979 graduate of Yale Law School.

Nature-Friendly Ordinances: Local Measures to Conserve Biodiversity

Table of Contents

Chapter Six—Growth Management and Infrastructure Ordinances

Chapter Seven—Conservation Practice Ordinances

Chapter Eight—Public Open Space Acquisition and Management

Chapter Nine—Conclusion

Chapter One—Introduction

Throughout the United States, local governments have begun to recognize responsibilities relating to the health and function of the natural environments within their boundaries. Land use ordinances—including planning, zoning, and subdivision regulations—must in many places address issues of habitat conservation, ecological function, watershed management, and conservation of diverse plants and animals. Unfortunately these objectives are understood by many elected officials and land use planners far less well than are economic development strategies, community design, and fiscal policy. There has been a long-standing disconnect between biological understanding and land use regulation.

But many local governments have begun to reconnect their interest in vibrant economic development with concern for healthy biological communities. At the same time, scientists have learned much about the requirements for functioning habitats. Land use planners and decisionmakers need access to this reliable information in order to be effective in conserving and restoring the lands and waters important for community well-being. The lessons of ecology and conservation biology can enable local decisionmakers to use their familiar land use tools more effectively—to make their development and redevelopment more "nature-friendly."

Throughout this book the term "biodiversity" is used to define the scope of living resources deserving consideration by local governments in setting the rules for development decisions. This relatively new term encompasses the "variety of living organisms and their populations, the genetic differences among them, and the natural communities and ecosystems in which they occur."[1] It provides a way of thinking systematically about the environment in which we live. By focusing on living organisms and systems, it avoids the pitfalls of prior concepts like "undeveloped land" or generalized references to "nature" or "natural resources."

Biodiversity places the emphasis upon *functioning systems* that sustain plants and animals, invertebrates, and microorganisms. A focus on biodiversity makes it possible for local governments to evaluate and employ tools that go beyond simply identifying and preserving a limited number of protected "critical areas" as their sole response to concerns about natural communities.[2] Biodiversity is a broader concept that requires consideration of the entire landscape, and it commands attention to those land management and development activities that occur outside specifically identified conservation areas as well as to those within such areas.

Local ordinances can contribute substantially to the conservation of biodiversity by supporting the creation and maintenance of conditions of ecological health on the local landscape. In order to do so, the ordinances must be based on well-understood ecological principles. They must also be congruent

1

with the other land management tools used by the local government. This book provides five key features to help ordinance drafters integrate these considerations into their many actions that affect land uses:

(1) Chapter Two defines the basic ecological guidelines that should guide land use decisionmaking by local governments. This brief list is based on the *Ecological Principles and Guidelines for Managing the Use of Land* (*Guidelines*), which was developed by a committee of the Ecological Society of America in 2000.[3] The Ecological Society of America is one of America's oldest and most respected scientific associations, representing biologists, ecologists, and other scientists working in the field of living organisms and their habitats. Its mission includes promoting ecological science by improving communication among ecologists; raising public awareness of the importance of ecological science; increasing the resources available for ecological science; and—in this context especially—ensuring the "appropriate use of ecological science in environmental decision making by enhancing communication between the ecological community and policy-makers."[4]

(2) Chapter Three identifies sources of biodiversity information and how such information can be used by local governments to improve their planning and ordinance drafting.

(3) Chapters Four through Eight explain how local governments can tailor familiar types of local land use regulations to apply the ecological principles to achieve desired results in local communities. The explanations describe how specific land use tools—comprehensive plans, overlay zones, resource protection ordinances, infrastructure requirements, subdivision regulations, acquisition programs, and many others—can serve specific conservation objectives.

(4) The discussion of each ordinance type identifies "key elements" essential for its effective use in conserving biodiversity.

(5) Each section of the book provides examples of specific local governments that have used these land use tools.[5] The selected examples provide context and informative experience, but they are not specifically intended as models for other communities whose conservation and development needs, ordinance styles, and institutional capacities may vary. Rather, the key elements are intended to serve that function.

Other Sources of Information

While attention to biodiversity by local governments is relatively new, this book joins several previous efforts that offer highly useful sources of information. Christopher Duerksen's excellent 1997 monograph for the American Planning Association, *Habitat Protection Planning: Where the Wild Things*

Are, identified ecological principles, types of local government tools, and some example communities.[6] Prof. John Nolon's recent book *Open Ground: Effective Local Strategies for Protecting Natural Resources*, published by the Environmental Law Institute (ELI) in 2003, organizes and collects local ordinances, plans, and strategies used by local governments across the United States to address a broad array of environmental issues, including but not limited to conservation of living resources.[7]

Additional knowledge and systematization of ecological principles have provided further insight into the opportunities for local action on biodiversity. More communities are seeking examples of how to apply this knowledge. Like Duerksen's monograph, this book focuses on local and regional biodiversity. However, this book is structured to discuss each ordinance type in far more detail in order to assist ordinance drafters. It also specifically relies on the *Guidelines* published in 2000.[8]

Like Professor Nolon's recent book, this book focuses on the content of ordinances, but it highlights the *key elements* of such ordinances that support biodiversity rather than providing sample ordinance language. This is based on the recognition that concepts, as well as models, are in short supply in the professional literature. As a land use planner in New Jersey told my ELI colleague Jessica Wilkinson: "We know how to write ordinances, we just need to know what to put in them." This new guidebook attempts to show what should go into them.

Use of the Guidebook

The leading causes of biodiversity loss and decline in the United States are the outright destruction of habitat and the impairment of habitat quality.[9] Many of these losses and impairments are the unintended byproducts of governmental and private decisions that failed to consider what is now known about ecological function. This guidebook will help communities avoid these unintended losses and take affirmative steps to conserve and restore those biodiversity features of their environment that add value regionally and locally.

The information in this guidebook is intended for all local decisionmakers that deal with the use of land. This includes local land use planning staff, planning and zoning boards, local legislative boards (councils, boards of commissioners, supervisors), and the many citizens and property owners across the country that participate in land use decisions that affect their communities. Participants in the critically important process of anticipating and shaping the character of development will find in this guidebook both a concise discussion of key ecological principles relevant to land use decisions and a ready reference to the tools to implement them.

The material that follows will help planners identify relevant biodiversity information, develop effective comprehensive plans that include biodiversity as a management element or objective, and prepare ordinances and amendments for consideration by the local legislative body. It will assist local elected officials and planning board members in evaluating and adopting amendments, plans, and ordinances, and in providing incentives or acquiring lands and interests in land where necessary. It will assist local officials in evaluating applications and making site plan and subdivision review decisions.

This guidebook will also be useful to citizen groups that are working to improve the quality of land use planning and decisions. Bringing the knowledge of ecology together with relevant land use tools will enable citizens to participate more effectively in the planning process and advocate changes to land use regulations and ordinances that will conserve the biodiversity of their communities.

Qualities of Effective Nature-Friendly Ordinances

Development regulations and land use plans must take the natural environment into account. They can deal with conservation of biodiversity. State enabling acts typically define the land use powers of local governments, and/or confer home-rule powers. In virtually all states there are explicit provisions in state law that recognize local government powers to conserve open space, natural resources, water quality, and provide in similar ways for the general welfare.[10] Some states have explicit requirements that such values be included in comprehensive plans and zoning ordinances, while others make such provisions permissive. Whatever the source, local governments exercise powers that can have a profound effect on the biological health of their lands and waters.

Identifying the powers of local governments is only the first step toward effective conservation. Selecting the right kind of tool for the task is critical. Areas important for biodiversity may be best protected through programs of land acquisition or through targeting of infrastructure spending. Other issues may be readily addressed through regulation. Judicial deference is most likely to be afforded to such local government actions when they are linked to enabling language, they are based on widely accepted scientific principles and understandings, and they are based on local studies and data that link the action to a defined problem.[11] The links need to be clearly drawn.

Land use plans and ordinances that take biodiversity into account are most likely to be effective when they reflect three understandings:

(1) First, they must articulate *clear standards* so that the goals, requirements, and rules are clearly understood. Vague generalities about concern for the natural environment expressed in a comprehensive plan, or ambiguous procedures or requirements in a zoning ordinance for reviewing development in areas of environmental concern, are both unlikely to result in effective implementation. The absence of clear goals and standards of performance leads to uncertainty. Where standards are vague, the ordinance becomes an obstacle and implementation becomes more difficult. This in turn makes the development process less fair, more costly, and unnecessarily complex. This guide shows that biodiversity-friendly ordinances can be as specific as ordinances that establish all kinds of other rules for development. Where the ordinance articulates the goals and the means, the entire community can ascertain

4

whether requirements are or are not being met, and land development interests can make decisions early in their planning processes that will benefit biodiversity.

(2) Second, the land use ordinance must reflect *public commitment to a plan* for the area. Where a vision of the future includes room for the biodiversity of a community, people will support it. Public commitment to this vision then helps ensure accountability in implementation and the stability of the land use regime. Specifically, it reduces the pressure for rezonings, special exceptions, and approval of poorly thought-out development plans. Local public commitment to a biodiversity plan can also help sustain private, voluntary, and even state and federal actions that support the attainment of the local objectives. This guide identifies some examples of instances where local commitment to a biodiversity goal, and its embodiment in an ordinance, attracted support from beyond the local government—in the form of funding, assistance, and compatible actions by other governmental and nongovernmental entities. These additional actions do not always occur but they are far more likely where the public commitment has been part of the ordinance process.

(3) Third, *political leadership* is important. Often a community will realize that an investment in its biodiversity future is possible only after an elected official or planning commissioner articulates why attention to these community assets is important. Making the political case is essential in order to lay the groundwork for effective planning, enactment of ordinances, and implementation. Many of the communities highlighted in this guide have one or more visionary leaders to thank for their progress. Sometimes the ordinance began as the vision of a single person in the local government; other times it came as the result of an education process begun by citizens outside of government; and in still others it was the creative local response to a state-initiated mandate—but a response that saw opportunity where others saw only obligation. The benefits of taking action must be clearly defined and explained to the public before the public will reciprocate with enthusiastic support for the action.

Chapter One Endnotes

1. KEYSTONE CENTER, KEYSTONE DIALOGUE ON BIOLOGICAL DIVERSITY ON FEDERAL LANDS (1991).

2. The critical areas concept has remained influential in land use decisionmaking. The identification of "areas of critical state concern" was an important innovation in AMERICAN LAW INSTITUTE, A MODEL LAND DEVELOPMENT CODE (1976), and "critical and sensitive areas" remain at the core of the American Planning Association's recent model state code provisions to enable local governments to address environmental concerns in land use regulation. *Special and Environmental Land Development Regulations and Land Use Incentives, in* GROWING SMART LEGISLATIVE GUIDEBOOK ch. 9 (Stuart Meck ed., American Planning Ass'n 2002).

3. Virginia H. Dale et al., *Ecological Principles and Guidelines for Managing the Use of Land*, 10 ECOLOGICAL APPLICATIONS 639 (2000) (also published in abridged form as ECOLOGICAL SOCIETY OF AMERICA'S COMMITTEE ON LAND USE, ECOLOGICAL PRINCIPLES AND GUIDELINES FOR MANAGING THE USE OF LAND (2000)).

4. Ecological Society of America, *About ESA, at* http://www.esa.org/aboutesa/ (last visited Dec. 1, 2003).

5. The intention has been to identify communities other than those discussed elsewhere in the planning literature. Thus, for example, as much as the author commends the well-designed transfer of development rights program in the New Jersey Pinelands, he has gone elsewhere for an example of this tool.

6. CHRISTOPHER DUERKSEN ET AL., HABITAT PROTECTION PLANNING: WHERE THE WILD THINGS ARE (Planning Advisory Service Report No. 470/471) (American Planning Ass'n 1997).

7. JOHN NOLON, OPEN GROUND: EFFECTIVE LOCAL STRATEGIES FOR PROTECTING NATURAL RESOURCES (Envtl. L. Inst. 2003).

8. Virginia Dale and Richard Haeuber's excellent *Applying Ecological Principles to Land Management* uses case studies to examine the interplay of public and private decisions with the *Guidelines* in various settings including the United States and India, but its focus is broader than ordinance drafting and the role of local governments. APPLYING ECOLOGICAL PRINCIPLES TO LAND MANAGEMENT (Virginia Dale & Richard Haeuber eds., Springer-Verlag 2001).

9. BRUCE STEIN ET AL., PRECIOUS HERITAGE: THE STATUS OF BIODIVERSITY IN THE UNITED STATES 242 (Oxford Univ. Press 2000). *See also* ELI, CONSERVATION THRESHOLDS FOR LAND USE PLANNERS (Envtl. L. Inst. 2003), *available at* http://www.elistore.org/reports_detail.asp?ID=10839 (last visited Dec. 1, 2003).

10. ELI & DEFENDERS OF WILDLIFE, PLANNING FOR BIODIVERSITY: AUTHORITIES IN STATE LAND USE LAWS (2003), *available at* http://www.elistore.org/reports_detail.asp?ID=10917 (last visited Dec. 1, 2003).

11. JOHN NOLON, NEW GROUND: THE ADVENT OF LOCAL ENVIRONMENTAL LAW 20-21 (Envtl. L. Inst. 2003).

Chapter Two—Conservation Guidelines for Land Use Ordinances

Scientists have made a great deal of progress in recent times in understanding how common land use choices affect conservation of biological diversity and the protection of ecological functions on the landscape. But local land use decisionmakers need to have this information in a form that they can use. Few planners and officials have time to make themselves masters of ecological science while performing their day jobs. And of those few with such knowledge, very few have time to recreate or summarize ecological learning for colleagues and constituents in a manner that will support decisions. Without a simple and accurate summary of current science, people may make decisions that reflect things they heard in school decades ago, or they may decide simply to forego dealing with an issue that appears complex.

Much has changed even since the 1960s and early 1970s when local land use regulations first began to take into account the conservation needs of communities as well as their development goals. Many of the conservation lessons that were understood then are still right, but others have been shown to be wrong. For instance, large-lot zoning was seen some decades ago as a tool of choice for wildlife and forest conservation. Science has now shown that large-lot zoning often creates only the semblance of a wildlife habitat and forest without the function. Fragmentation of the habitat into separate two-acre or five-acre parcels has profoundly adverse and widespread effects even though the footprint of each physically disturbed area may be small. Similarly, decades ago wildlife biologists urged the creation and maintenance of more "edge" habitat (the margin of forest with field, for example) because edges tended to have more mammals and birds and larger aggregate numbers of species. Now it is well understood that edge habitat is good for some species (like deer, raccoons, cowbirds) and bad for others (such as forest-nesting migratory songbirds), and that the effects of the edge can be quite negative for some species even at a substantial distance away from the habitat edge.

The point is not to suggest that edge or large lots are always bad but to acknowledge that ecological science has given us tools to approach land use regulation with greater sophistication and precision than we could previously. One would scarcely practice medicine today using the state of medical knowledge in 1970—although even that would be preferable to no medicine at all. Similarly, land use planners should use the best biological understanding available today rather than rely on general assumptions about "open space" and habitat goals articulated in connection with 1970s-era planning innovations.

Conservation biology is a relatively recent field of scientific knowledge that seeks to discover the relationships between biology and the landscape, and to apply them to achieve conservation goals.[1] It applies scientific knowledge

7

about habitat requirements, population biology, genetics, ethology, plant biology, ecological systems, soil science, hydrology, and related disciplines. Conservation biology and its related disciplines provide land use planners and officials with some basic tools that they can use in designing and administering ordinances governing land use and development.

Among the related disciplines is ecology. Ecology focuses on the natural systems and processes (including nutrient cycling and energy flows) that affect the landscape upon which life depends. The Ecological Society of America's Committee on Land Use recently distilled scientific understandings about these processes into a series of guidelines and recommendations for land use decisions.[2] This chapter draws on these guidelines and related scientific literature to articulate a limited set of conservation guidelines for those involved in the land use regulatory process. This chapter also draws upon additional lessons from conservation biology that have been generally recognized as guides for landscape management decisions.[3] There are two overarching guidelines and eight more specific land use guidelines.

Overarching Guidelines

It is important to examine proposed local decisions in two dimensions—the larger *regional landscape* and the potential effect of *changes in ecosystems over time*.[4] Planners and officials should always examine these two dimensions of their decisions as early in the process as possible.

Examine Impacts of Local Decisions in a Regional Context

Ecological communities of plants, wildlife, and the ecosystems on which they rely are not coextensive with political boundaries. Yet they are strongly influenced by actions that occur within a single political jurisdiction. In considering a land use decision, planners should identify the surrounding region that is likely to interact with the biologically significant areas within their legal borders. Conversely, they should identify the areas external to their jurisdiction that will be affected by their proposed decision.[5] They should also examine how adjoining jurisdictions are using and managing their lands and waters. Without this broader review, it will be difficult to predict the beneficial and adverse effects of land use decisions by the community, and it will not be possible to tailor local actions to larger ecosystem needs.

There is a substantial disconnect between the scale at which we need to plan and manage to effectively conserve biodiversity and the scale at which land use planning and decisionmaking is traditionally done.[6] Of course, the land use regulatory scale will vary from state to state. Some states provide for planning and zoning and land use regulation at the township and municipal level, others by county governments. But, in general, the relevant area in which biodiversity needs to be understood will almost always be larger than one political jurisdiction. At least it frequently overlaps the boundaries of any one jurisdiction.

This spatial mismatch does not mean that resource protection can be ignored, nor that it can be left entirely to the state or federal governments. In the United States, land use powers reside at the local level. It is essential to use these powers in a way that takes the larger landscape into account. Declining to do so will relegate biodiversity to continued decline and will limit local planning for biodiversity to small systems of disconnected parks and overlay zones. Even though land use regulation is effectively limited to land use *within* the relevant political jurisdiction—as it almost always is, with the exception of those localities in a few states that have limited extraterritorial land use jurisdiction—the local jurisdiction should consider the effects of its actions on the larger biological landscape.

State agencies and conservation organizations often have information on the habitat needs of particular species. Some have identified watersheds or ecological regions that require particular attention. This information helps local communities assess the likely impact of their decisions over a larger area. Assessment of impacts, in turn, makes it possible for planners to incorporate this regional information into the local action and thereby make it more effective. Failing to identify the relevant ecological community and its stressors may result in the adoption of a local plan that has no chance of biological success. Conversely, failure to examine regional factors may lead to the adoption of land use constraints that are not necessary given the regional context.

Examine Impacts of Local Decisions Over Time, Considering Foreseeable Future Changes in the Landscape

Ecological systems and landscapes change over time. The Ecological Society of America recommends that land use planners plan for "long-term change."[7] Planners must take into account the fact that landscapes change and evolve over time: forests mature, lakes fill in, tornadoes create gaps and openings, beaches erode, domestic animals affect the population of wild animals, etc. Thus, planners must take into account the likely future condition of the ecosystem or landscape when making decisions and not simply assume that an area set aside as a bog will remain a bog without regard to changes in surrounding land uses, or that a habitat area for a particular species will always be occupied by the same species. It is essential to consider likely future changes on the landscape and the cumulative effects of adjacent land uses as well. Just as planners must make long-term projections about human population, economic development, infrastructure needs, water consumption, traffic, and other factors in order to plan effectively, so too do they need to plan for long-term landscape function.

These two overarching guidelines apply to every land use decision. Planners should attempt to put the pending decision into the larger regional context in order to understand its effect on biodiversity. Even a small project (an office park, a road deicing maintenance facility), if sited in the wrong place, can have a profoundly negative regional effect. Conversely, protection of a core feature (the recharge area for a spring system, the core habitat of a threatened bat, the headwaters of a regionally important urban stream) can have profoundly positive effects in the larger landscape context.

Planners also should determine whether the land use decision being made today takes into account the fact that lands and biological communities change over time. They are subject to foreseeable natural and human-caused stresses that must be accommodated in some fashion. Effective planning for biodiversity conservation, like human place-making in the planning profession, recognizes that ecology—like human communities—is dynamic. Biologically sensitive planning is not the creation and maintenance of the landscape equivalent of a static museum diorama.

These overarching guidelines are as important for the planner from a small, older township as they are for the staff of a large rapidly developing county. Actions always affect landscapes, not just parcels. And good decisions attempt to anticipate future events, not assume that tomorrow will be just like yesterday.

Guidelines for Land Use Decisions

The following eight guidelines provide a checklist of practical choices that can improve the effect of local land use decisionmaking on the living environment. They are not prescriptive but do indicate which practices are more likely rather than less likely to support biodiversity conservation.[8]

Guidelines

1. Maintain large areas of contiguous habitat and avoid fragmenting these areas.
2. Maintain meaningful connections between habitat areas.
3. Protect rare landscape elements, sensitive areas, and associated species.
4. Allow natural patterns of disturbance to continue in order to maintain diversity and resilience of habitat types.
5. Minimize the introduction and spread of non-native species and favor native plants and animals.
6. Minimize human introduction of nutrients, chemicals, and pollutants.
7. Avoid land uses that deplete natural resources over a broad area.
8. Compensate for adverse effects of development on natural processes.

---

1. Maintain Large Areas of Contiguous Habitat and Avoid Fragmenting These Areas

Large habitat areas are important to maintaining key organisms and ecosystem processes. First, larger patches of habitat generally reflect greater species diversity than smaller patches of the same habitat. Larger patches have more local environmental variability, such as differences in microclimate, more structural variation in plants and vegetation, and greater diversity of topographic features, which provide more opportunities for organisms with different requirements and tolerances to find suitable sites within the patch.[9] Larger patches also tend to have greater species diversity because they contain a greater abundance of interior habitat than small patches, which often will contain only "edge" habitat. Interior and edge habitat can be very different, in terms of their exposure to pollution, sunlight, predators, habitat disturbance, roads, and other effects, therefore supporting different organisms. Larger patches, containing both interior and edge species, are more reliably diverse than smaller patches that often contain only edge species.[10] Larger patches are also better able to support species requiring larger home ranges, helping to conserve species such as large mammals that require greater areas to meet their food, water, and territorial needs than small habitat areas can provide.

Second, large habitat areas often contain a greater number of individuals of any species than smaller areas, due to the greater availability of food, nest sites, territory, and other resources in the patch. Larger populations tend to be more viable and persistent than smaller populations. Smaller populations are more vulnerable to extinction due to environmental fluctuations, demographic variation, inbreeding, and reduced gene pools.[11]

Avoidance of habitat fragmentation is equally important. Habitat fragmentation is a major cause of the loss of biodiversity, as it not only reduces overall habitat area, but also facilitates predation and disease and creates barriers to migration that reduce natural communities' resiliency.[12] *See* Figure 1. Habitat fragmentation is understood to operate with "threshold" dynamics. This means that although gradual reduction of contiguous habitat may have gradual effects on the presence or abundance of a species, once the threshold is passed, the adverse effects can be dramatic. These land-cover changes are most likely to have substantial effects on species when habitat is low to intermediate in abundance. Under these conditions, small changes in habitat abundance may cause the connectivity threshold to be passed with strongly adverse effects on the species population.[13]

Figure 1: Habitat Fragmentation

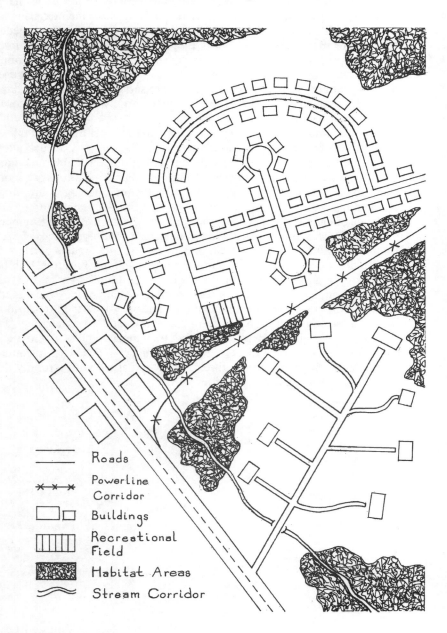

Roads

Powerline
Corridor

Buildings

Recreational
Field

Habitat Areas

Stream Corridor

Drawing by Kathryn Hubler

In order to minimize the threats from habitat fragmentation, it is critical to maintain habitat large enough to protect species of concern. The habitat areas should be large enough to maintain the minimum territories of the species, where possible, especially for species at the top of the food chain. Moreover, it is important to try to minimize edge and fragmentation effects. For example, conserved areas can be configured in more rounded parcels in order to minimize edge-to-area ratios and avoiding internal fragmentation by roads and fences. Communities should work to aggregate small nature reserves into larger conservation blocks to facilitate gene flow and migration among populations and to ensure adequate representation of species and habitats. Communities can also link protected areas with habitat corridors to foster connectivity among habitats.[14]

The importance of large areas does not negate the role of small areas nor does it absolve small local governmental jurisdictions from attention to this guideline. Small jurisdictions may contain portions of a larger habitat or may provide a crucial connection between larger habitat areas. Moreover, understanding the importance of conserving contiguous habitat areas can help a local government decide how to configure its design of a park, an overlay zone, or even a construction project on a brownfields site.

2. Maintain Meaningful Connections Between Habitat Areas

Many species require movement during their life cycles for persistence and survival. This can include daily movement within the home range for food, water, shelter, and escape from predators. It includes migration, in which certain species travel seasonally between breeding grounds and primary feeding areas. It includes metamorphosis, in which certain species must move from one habitat to another during the course of the life cycle. And it includes dispersal of both plants and animals, which allows a population to shift or extend its range, thereby increasing its resiliency in the face of ecosystem change.[15]

Maintaining large contiguous habitat areas is the single best way to ensure adequate species movement. However, population growth and related urban expansion and development have fragmented habitat and thus severely disrupted species movement in many areas. Primary barriers to movement include land conversion from natural habitats to developed environments, with their associated roads, power lines, noise, heat, and pollution.[16]

Where habitat areas have been fragmented, it is important to minimize the distance between protected habitats in order to ensure species movement. The distance between habitats and the nature of the transitional or connecting habitat between these separate areas influence the persistence of species.[17] It is important to locate conserved habitat areas in close proximity rather than widely spaced apart. Minimizing the distance also means increasing the permeability of existing barriers to movement between habitats. For example, roads block the movement of small animals and serve as the primary source of mortality for wide-ranging mammals. To reduce these effects, roads can be sited away from movement corridors, nonessential roads can be closed or limited in some natural areas, and design features such as underpasses and overpasses can be used to enable wildlife to safely cross highways.[18] Fences, like roads, also tend to restrict species movement and can be eliminated, minimized, or substituted for by "living" fences or shrubs that are more porous. Other barriers to movement can be minimized by, for example, designing powerline rights-of-way to include wildlife crossings, reducing the width of such rights-of-way, and leaving forest connections intact in some of the stream valleys or other depressions over which such rights-of-way pass.

In addition to avoiding barriers and making barriers more permeable to species movement, it is also desirable to affirmatively link habitats by identifying and conserving wildlife corridors. Corridors such as riparian zones—vegetated strips and floodplains adjacent to rivers and streams—can effectively link populations from otherwise disconnected habitats. This may help to minimize local extirpations and genetic isolation of wildlife populations. When placed along migration routes, conservation corridors may help to ensure adequate movement of species to meet their food, cover, and breeding requirements at different times of the year.

Scientific information should be used to design corridors that provide meaningful and healthy connections between larger habitat areas. *See* Figure 2. Corridors must be designed and managed to establish meaningful connections between habitat areas. For example, an intensively developed bicycle path greenway may not serve as an effective habitat corridor if it consists entirely of paved surfaces and mowed shoulders and berms. Some corridors can also have negative effects if they facilitate the spread of non-native species and disease to the detriment of isolated populations of native species.[19] Corridors often require active management to assure that they maintain their biological function.

Figure 2: Habitat Corridors

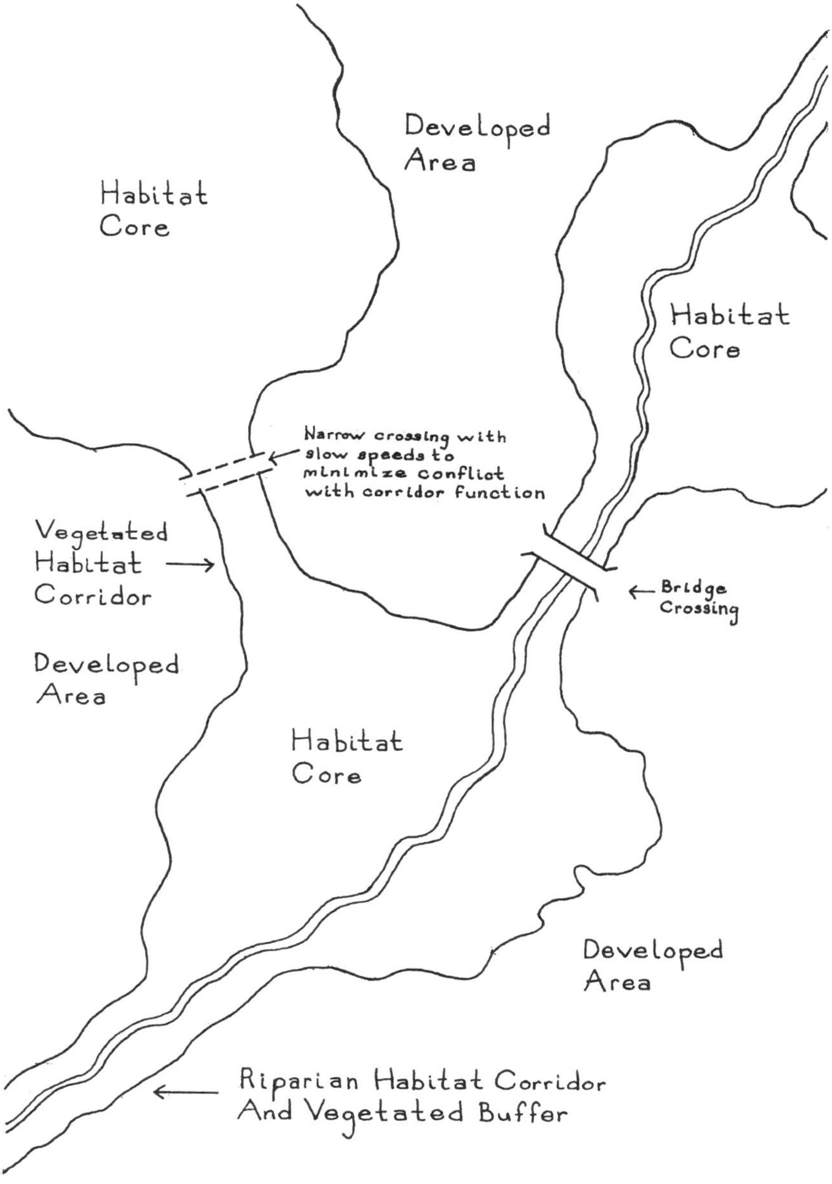

Developed
Area

Habitat
Core

Habitat
Core

Narrow crossing with
slow speeds to
minimize conflict
with corridor function

Vegetated
Habitat →
Corridor

Bridge
Crossing ←

Developed
Area

Habitat
Core

Developed
Area

Riparian Habitat Corridor
And Vegetated Buffer ←

Drawing by Kathryn Hubler

3. Protect Rare Landscape Elements, Sensitive Areas, and Associated Species

The ecological importance of certain habitat areas may be much greater than suggested by their spatial extent. While rare landscape elements such as wetlands, watercourses, floodplains, or steep slopes may occupy a small area of land, they are frequently of high importance for a region's biodiversity. Rare landscape elements typically contribute a disproportionate share to the diversity of wildlife found in a given place. For example, in the southern Appalachian Mountains, 84% of the federally listed threatened and endangered terrestrial plant and animal species occur in rare ecological communities.[20] In order to protect these habitats, rare landscape elements need to be identified, usually via an inventory and analysis of vegetation types, hydrology, soils, physical features, and associated species.[21] Because habitat diversity is markedly reduced if rare landscape features are lost, it is important to focus conservation efforts on these critical areas and guide development toward areas with more common landscape features.

4. Allow Natural Patterns of Disturbance to Continue in Order to Maintain Diversity and Resilience of Habitat Types

Periodic disturbances such as storms, floods, and fires play an important role in maintaining patches in various stages and in maintaining the native plants and animals that co-evolved under the influence of those natural processes.[22] For example, "periodic burning and grazing is needed to maintain native species in tallgrass prairie, and ground fires are needed to ensure regeneration of oak forests." Without these disturbances, habitat can be lost through "natural processes of succession no matter how well it is protected from human use."[23]

Because these disturbances are ecologically important, it is sometimes not enough to simply leave nature alone. In other words, passive protection of habitat may not be enough. Where sources of natural disturbance have not been maintained, it may be necessary to emulate them to maintain the plants and animals native to those landscapes. "Prescribed burns might take the place of natural fires, logging might be used to simulate natural canopy gaps, livestock could serve as a surrogate for absent native herbivores, and releases of water from impoundments can be timed to mimic natural runoff."[24]

In order to allow these natural (or if necessary, emulated) disturbance patterns to take place, decisionmakers must ensure that these disturbances do not lead to catastrophic societal problems. Unfortunately, the continued expansion of human settlement in disturbance-prone landscapes is likely to result in increased conflicts between human needs and the maintenance of disturbance regimes necessary to sustain ecosystems. Therefore, land use plans must account for the occurrences and impacts of these disturbances.[25] For example, regulations must prohibit building on floodplains, account for sufficient buffer zones surrounding floodplains, avoid land use changes that affect natural water drainage, and prohibit building in fire-prone areas.

5. Minimize the Introduction and Spread of Non-Native Species and Favor Native Plants and Animals

Native plants and animals have great value, as they represent the conditions that co-evolved with the landscape. They are uniquely adapted to their surroundings, and they affect ecosystem processes and the persistence and viability of other plants and animals native to the area.

Introduction of non-native species can severely disrupt natural conditions and species composition in an area.[26] Non-native species (and particularly invasive exotic species) can alter community composition and ecosystem processes via their roles as competitors, predators, pathogens, or vectors of disease, as well as through effects on water balance, biological productivity, and habitat structure. Non-natives can even assume a dominant role, reducing the abundance of native species and creating conditions under which other non-native species can more easily spread.[27]

Non-native species are often introduced by changes in land use associated with land parcelization and development. Exurban development can promote the introduction of non-native species used for landscaping and can increase the abundance of roadways and other corridors that facilitate the spread of non-native species. Non-native plants and invertebrates as well as diseases can also be transported and spread by vehicles or boats.

In order to conserve, restore, or maintain a landscape of native species, native plant species should be planted in lieu of non-native species in urban, suburban, and other developed areas and should be used in public and private infrastructure projects whenever possible. Native species frequently become established more readily and require less maintenance than non-natives. Native species are also adapted to long-term variations in climate or disturbance regimes to which non-native species sometimes succumb. Maintaining the environmental conditions associated with native species may also limit the proliferation of non-natives.[28] Non-native plant species can be uprooted or otherwise eradicated to prevent their spread.

In addition, other preventative mechanisms can be taken to reduce the spread of non-natives. For example, the U.S. Forest Service has found that cleaning trucks or minimizing traffic in some sensitive areas during wet periods can greatly reduce the transport of certain forest pathogens.[29] Also, in order to minimize impact on native fauna, dogs and cats can be prevented from roaming freely, and garbage and other potential domestic food sources for native animals (such as bears) can be controlled to avoid fatal conflicts with domestic animals and human habitation.

6. Minimize Human Introduction of Nutrients, Chemicals, and Pollutants

Introduced compounds can directly impair biodiversity by killing terrestrial and aquatic species, by hindering their reproduction, or by changing their food supply. Such substances, which may originate from agricultural use, intensive urbanization, suburban development, lawn maintenance activities, municipal landfills, leaking underground storage tanks, failing septic systems, golf courses, and industrial activities, have drastic indirect effects as well. Some can cause reduced reproductive success and lower survival rates, disrupt the species composition of an area, or cause birth defects. For example, the input of large amounts of sediment and associated agricultural chemicals in many rivers and streams has caused a drastic decline in aquatic diversity.[30] Excess nutrients have resulted in drastic diminution of fish and invertebrate populations, with corresponding adverse effects on water-dependent terrestrial organisms. To minimize the effects of these harmful substances, it is critical to minimize applications and discharges where possible as well as to maintain buffer strips and vegetative areas surrounding wetlands and watercourses that can act as filters for pollutants.

7. Avoid Approving Land Uses That Deplete Natural Resources Over a Broad Area

Depletion of natural resources—such as soil, water, and forests—can disrupt natural processes in ways that often are not reversible over fairly long periods of time. This guideline is aimed at major activities that can have long-term effects on underlying resources such as soil and groundwater. For example, some forms of intensive agriculture if conducted on highly erodible soils and steep slopes can result in the loss of substantial volumes of topsoil, which takes many years to regenerate. This may result in lands that cannot be restored to ecological productivity over the long term. Some logging practices, including overlarge clearcuts on very steep slopes, diameter-limit cutting of only the most profitable trees while leaving weaker trees for regeneration, and use of heavy equipment without adequate care for forest soils, can also have long-term ill effects on water quality and soils as well as impair the future forest resource. A community's overreliance on private wells and septic systems to support sprawling residential development in areas of limited water supply can result in difficulties both for long-term human water supplies and for the ability of an aquifer to recharge and support local springs, surface waters, and other waterway systems important for the local ecology. Similarly, allowing the paving over of large areas adjacent to stream banks can have lasting adverse effects on water quality, hydrology, habitat, and aquatic species.

In order to minimize natural resource depletion, it is important to first determine what resources are at risk. For example, in many parts of the United States, water is a scarce natural resource that should be carefully used to ensure the long-term health of both the human community and the ecosystem. Heavily water-consuming developments and industries may be incompatible with the resource's availability.[31] Growth must be compatible with the availability of water, healthy soils, forests, and other resources. It is important to avoid inappropriate land uses that deplete these natural resources over broad areas.

8. Compensate for Adverse Effects of Development on Natural Processes

Wherever possible, development should be designed to avoid negative effects on natural processes.[32] However, if authorized development may lead to losses of biological diversity, compensation through restoration measures within the same landscape is necessary and appropriate. Thus, wetland mitigation and restoration requirements can help to serve the objective of "no net loss" of wetlands in a given landscape.[33] On-the-ground compensation for other habitat losses by creation or protection of habitat areas can also help alleviate unavoidable impacts. It is important to recognize, however, that mitigation may not adequately replace or restore all functions and values of natural systems. Where compensatory mitigation is used to offset habitat loss, it is important to monitor mitigation sites to ensure that the desired ecosystem functions are being achieved.[34]

Conclusion

Local governments need rules of thumb to guide their thinking about conservation. Ordinances can only be "nature-friendly" if there is some content to the concept.

Thinking about the larger regional landscape and about natural and social change over time are both critical overarching concepts. A municipality that attempts to conduct conservation without looking over its borders is less likely to succeed than a municipality with a greater sense of the regional resource. A municipality that plans for the longer term is more likely to succeed than one that views its comprehensive plan (or the natural resources element of its plan) as a static exercise.

The eight guidelines expressing current ecological knowledge and conservation biology precepts will help local governments make the more detailed decisions—decisions about how to design zoning districts, what infrastructure plans to adopt, what subdivision regulations to apply, how to manage municipally owned lands in a sensitive way, and many others. Put them on a card and carry them in your pocket, put them in the principles section of the natural resources element of your comprehensive plan, use them as guiding principles for your planning staff and your public works department. Make science-based decisions. We have the capacity to do so.

Chapter Two Endnotes

1. The term "conservation biology" began to be used in the early 1980s. Michael E. Soule, *What Is Conservation Biology?*, 35 BIOSCIENCE 727 (1985). The Society for Conservation Biology was founded in 1985 and began publishing its scholarly journal *Conservation Biology* in 1987.

2. Virginia H. Dale et al., *Ecological Principles and Guidelines for Managing the Use of Land*, 10 ECOLOGICAL APPLICATIONS 639 (2000) (also published in abridged form as ECOLOGICAL SOCIETY OF AMERICA'S COMMITTEE ON LAND USE, ECOLOGICAL PRINCIPLES AND GUIDELINES FOR MANAGING THE USE OF LAND (2000)).

3. REED NOSS & ALAN COOPERRIDER, SAVING NATURE'S LEGACY: PROTECTING AND RESTORING BIODIVERSITY (Island Press 1994); RICHARD B. PRIMACK, ESSENTIALS OF CONSERVATION BIOLOGY (Sinauer Associates Publishers 1993). These conservation biology guidelines have been compiled in previous Environmental Law Institute (ELI) publications including JESSICA B. WILKINSON & ELI, PROTECTING DELAWARE'S NATURAL HERITAGE: TOOLS FOR BIODIVERSITY CONSERVATION (Envtl. L. Inst. 1999); ELI, INDIANA'S BIOLOGICAL DIVERSITY: STRATEGIES AND TOOLS FOR CONSERVATION (Envtl. L. Inst. 1995); and ELI, OHIO'S BIOLOGICAL DIVERSITY: STRATEGIES AND TOOLS FOR CONSERVATION (Envtl. L. Inst. 1998) [hereinafter ELI, OHIO'S BIOLOGICAL DIVERSITY]. For ELI state biodiversity publications, see http://www.elistore.org/reports_list.asp?topic=Biodiversity (last visited Dec. 1, 2003).

4. The Ecological Society of America articulates four "principles" that are reflected in these two overarching guidelines:

    (1) Place Principle—"Local climatic, hydrologic, edaphic, and geomorphologic factors as well as biotic interactions strongly affect ecological processes and the abundance and distribution of species at any one place."
    (2) Species Principle—"Particular species and networks of interacting species have key, broad-scale ecosystem-level effects."
    (3) Time Principle—"Ecological processes function at many time scales, some long, some short; and ecosystems change through time."
    (4) Disturbance Principle—"The type, intensity, and duration of disturbance shape the characteristics of populations, communities, and ecosystems."

    Dale et al., *supra* note 2, at 649-56.

5. *Id.* at 656-58.

6. *See* James M. McElfish Jr., *Learning From the Past and Looking Toward the Future*, *in* JOHN NOLON, NEW GROUND: THE ADVENT OF LOCAL ENVIRONMENTAL LAW 399-404 (Envtl. L. Inst. 2003) (discussing the jurisdictional mismatch and solutions available in land use law).

7. Dale et al., *supra* note 2, at 659.

8. Although the land use guidelines are principally drawn from the ecological guidelines developed by the Ecological Society of America's Land Use Committee, several have been expanded in recognition of related conservation biology principles, e.g., Guideline 6 reflects specific concerns that relate to the Ecological Society of America's guideline to "implement land use practices that are compatible" with an area's "natural potential."

9. Dale et al., *supra* note 2, at 655.

10. *Id.*

11. PRIMACK, *supra* note 3; NOSS & COOPERRIDER, *supra* note 3, at 59-62; *see also* ELI, OHIO'S BIOLOGICAL DIVERSITY, *supra* note 3, at 22.

12. NOSS & COOPERRIDER, *supra* note 3, at 51-57.

13. Dale et al., *supra* note 2, at 655.

14. NOSS & COOPERRIDER, *supra* note 3, at 150-56; *see also* ELI, OHIO'S BIOLOGICAL DIVERSITY, *supra* note 3, at 25.

15. SHEILA PECK, PLANNING FOR BIODIVERSITY 73-75 (Island Press 1998).

16. *Id.* at 76.

17. Leonard F. Ruggiero et al., *Viability Analysis in Biological Evacuations: Concepts of Population Viability Analysis, Biological Population, and Ecological Scale*, 8 CONSERVATION BIOLOGY 364-72 (1994).

18. PECK, *supra* note 15, at 76-77.

19. Dale et al., *supra* note 2, at 660.

20. *Id.* at 659.

21. *Id.*

22. WALTER REID & KENTON MILLER, KEEPING OPTIONS ALIVE: THE SCIENTIFIC BASIS FOR CONSERVING BIODIVERSITY (World Resources Institute 1989); NOSS & COOPERRIDER, *supra* note 3, at 43-46.

23. CHRISTOPHER DUERKSEN ET AL., HABITAT PROTECTION PLANNING: WHERE THE WILD THINGS ARE 15 (Planning Advisory Service Report No. 470/471) (American Planning Ass'n 1997).

24. *Id.*

25. Dale et al., *supra* note 2, at 659.

26. MEG FILBEY ET AL., HALTING THE INVASION: STATE TOOLS FOR INVASIVE SPECIES MANAGEMENT (Envtl. L. Inst. 2002), *available at* http://www.elistore.org/reports_detail.asp?ID=10678 (last visited Dec. 1, 2003).

27. Dale et al., *supra* note 2, at 660-61.

28. *Id.* at 661.

29. *Id.* at 660.

30. *See generally* U.S. GEOLOGICAL SURVEY, NATIONAL WATER QUALITY ASSESSMENT (2001 and updates), *available at* http://water.usgs.gov/nawqa (last visited Dec. 1, 2003). *See also* ELI, OHIO'S BIOLOGICAL DIVERSITY, *supra* note 3, at 24.

31. Dale et al., *supra* note 2, at 659-60.

32. *Id.* at 661.

33. *See* ENVIRONMENTAL LAW INSTITUTE, BANKS AND FEES: THE STATUS OF OFF-SITE WETLAND MITIGATION IN THE UNITED STATES (2002), *available at* http://www.elistore.org/reports_detail.asp?ID=10695 (last visited Dec. 1, 2003).

34. COMMISSION ON ENVIRONMENTAL QUALITY, OFFICE OF THE PRESIDENT, BIODIVERSITY ON PRIVATE LANDS (Commission on Environmental Quality 1993).

Chapter Three—Information for Local Conservation

Local governments use many legal tools to address land use, growth, and development issues. With sufficient information, these can be designed and implemented to support biodiversity conservation as an additional goal important to communities' long-term well-being. Reliable information can help communities:

- recognize the need for conservation;
- identify sources of locally useful biodiversity information; and
- select the appropriate planning or regulatory tool.

Need for Conservation

Many local governments have broadly identified natural resources as an important part of their land use objectives.[1] Others have not done so because their land use plans have not been updated for many years, because they have no land use regulations other than subdivision ordinances that do not address policy objectives, or because they have not examined available information to determine that important natural resources exist.

The increasing trend is to include natural resources (including plant and animal communities) in planning and in land use regulation. In 2000, for example, Pennsylvania enacted amendments to its statewide municipal plan enabling legislation requiring all comprehensive plans to include a plan for "the protection of natural and historic resources to the extent not preempted by federal or state law . . . includ[ing] but not limited to, wetlands and aquifer recharge zones, woodlands, steep slopes, prime agricultural land, flood plains [sic], unique natural areas[,] and historic sites."[2] This is not a new idea for planners. Indeed, University of Pennsylvania Prof. Ian McHarg's influential book, *Design With Nature*, published in 1969, led to many communities realizing that their development choices were intertwined with their environmental features and that good planning required consideration of the natural landscape and its functions.[3]

In many states, revisions to state planning laws in the 1970s and 1980s led to local plans and ordinances intended to protect critical areas, wetlands, floodplains, groundwater, steep slopes, and habitats.[4] Still more recently, communities have begun to identify the substantial natural resource values that add to land values, quality of life, and ecological services (such as the flood control benefits of wetlands and the water quality benefits of forested watersheds).[5]

A community may decide to pursue adoption of ordinances because of well-understood threats to the lands and waters on which the community depends (through uncontrolled development or planning mistakes that have become obvious over time), because of concern for particular high-profile areas (such as waterfronts, sand dunes, bogs, and raptor nesting areas), because of federal or state mandates (such as the federal Endangered Species Act (ESA)[6] or state critical areas laws), or because of interest on the part of local residents in improving the quality of local land regulation and capital improvement plans. Whatever the source of the interest, local governments will find it necessary to move rapidly beyond the generalized concept that natural resources are important and should be taken into account toward a plan to obtain reliable, verifiable information that can support decisions about threats, opportunities, and ways to serve multiple objectives.

Information for Action

Local land use regulations must be grounded in good information. This is as true of conservation information supporting nature-friendly ordinances as it is of traffic information supporting standards for the sizing of roads and placement of signals. Good professional practice requires a sound information basis for any local ordinance. Such information is also essential to assure that a measure will be legally sustainable if it should be challenged in court.

Just as a planning board needs information about projected population trends in the community, planned state infrastructure investments, and economic characteristics of its own and surrounding jurisdictions, so too must it understand the biological and ecological setting within which the community operates. Too frequently this task has been relegated simply to a quick check by a land use consultant (or developer seeking a rezoning) for the presence or absence of federally listed endangered species. And in many instances environmental information has been treated solely as a constraint, and not as an opportunity—much less a planning goal. Yet biodiversity information is highly useful in planning the future of a community—including status and trends in water quantity and quality, identification of habitat types, sensitive species, and plants and wildlife.

Before any discussion of plans and ordinances, local governments should begin by considering key information resources. Collecting baseline ecological information is a necessary and critical first step toward integrating biodiversity considerations into land use planning and decisionmaking. This information is needed not only for planning purposes, but can also help to test current ecological models and hypothesis, to identify areas for subsequent monitoring, and to identify areas in need of further research.[7]

However conducted, ecological information-gathering involves creating an up-to-date inventory of the community's ecological infrastructure and its associated components. Ecological information useful to the planning and ordinance-writing process includes data on soils, steep slopes, open space, wetlands, hydrology, the location of roads and other linear features, vegetation, water, wildlife, climate, and status and trends of change. Analysis of the data can determine the relevant stressors and needs of the ecosystem, including such issues as native versus invasive species, habitat patch sizes, migration routes, and buffer locations and sizes needed to maintain water quality and ecological integrity.

Information-gathering takes many forms and can produce many forms of information needed to support decisions. Sources of information can include data collection or assembly efforts specifically commissioned by local governments. But many existing sources of relevant conservation information are available.[8] Universities and other academic institutions can provide further information in many areas. Some states have constructed statewide ecological information systems and have made biodiversity conservation plans available to local governments to assist them in planning their own actions.[9]

Local governments seeking to integrate biodiversity conservation into their plans and ordinances should seek information that enables them to determine:

- whether there is a regional or state conservation plan that should inform their decisions;
- what living resources and ecosystems are present in the jurisdiction;
- whether there are any unique or unusual habitat areas within their jurisdictions;
- what opportunities may exist for restoration of living resources and ecosystem functions that previously were present in the jurisdiction but are currently absent or impaired;
- what landscape connections exist within the jurisdiction that may help connect habitat areas that lie fully or partly outside the jurisdiction;
- what areas are most important for conservation;
- whether rare, threatened, or endangered species may be conserved within the jurisdiction or through actions taken within the jurisdiction; and
- to what extent anticipated land uses and development decisions can be carried out in ways that also serve conservation goals.

State Biodiversity Information

At a minimum, every community can consult its state natural heritage program for information on endangered, threatened, rare, and vulnerable species and on unique plant and animal communities. Many of these programs also have basic information on ecological systems and types of natural communities present throughout the state. These programs operate in all 50 states and have in the aggregate nearly 800 staff. In many states they provide substantial data and conservation information in addition to threatened and endangered species occurrence information. These programs can be contacted through state natural resource agencies. The programs are also members of a network called NatureServe, and information about these programs can be accessed through the NatureServe website.[10]

A detailed discussion of the ways in which state laws and policies create demand for biodiversity and natural heritage information—and the ways in which such information is used—is found in the Environmental Law Institute's 2003 study, *Planning With Nature: Biodiversity Information in Action.*[11] The National Biological Information Infrastructure, a partnership of government agencies, private industry, nongovernmental organizations, and academic institutions, also provides access to state-by-state biodiversity information resources.[12]

Many states have established more planning-oriented sources of ecological information specifically intended for use by their local governments. For example, Pennsylvania has a "county natural area inventory program" that is producing biodiversity and habitat information for each county. About one-half of Pennsylvania's counties have completed these inventories, which are carried out on a cooperative basis by The Nature Conservancy and the Western Pennsylvania Conservancy. The inventories are intended to identify resources, habitats, species, and ecosystems of particular importance and to make such information available to planners and land use regulators in Pennsylvania's more than 2,500 local government units.

> The inventories contain information on the highest quality natural areas in the county, including mapping and a description of each site. General recommendations to help plan for the protection and continued existence of rare plants, animals, and natural communities also are included in these inventories.[13]

Maryland's Green Infrastructure[14] program and Florida's Greenways[15] program provide habitat and ecological information to communities on a statewide basis. Each of these programs includes maps that show areas of significance for conservation purposes, and each is available for use and consideration by local governments as they prepare their own plans and ordinances of numerous types.

To guide local land protection efforts and planning by its more than 500 separate towns, Massachusetts has expended $1.5 million in state bond money for geographic information system mapping of terrestrial biodiversity resources statewide. Massachusetts' statewide BioMap identifies those areas of the state most in need of protection to conserve biodiversity for future generations. These include identified core habitats and supporting natural landscape areas.[16] The BioMap guides communities, as well as the commonwealth itself, in making conservation acquisition decisions and in planning for future growth and development.[17] Massachusetts is engaged in follow-up work in mapping the aquatic biodiversity of the commonwealth in order to provide its local governments with detailed information on inland lakes, streams, ponds, vernal pools, and other freshwater systems.

State resources are particularly important to municipalities that have little in the way of professional planning staff or resources. The availability of state information can assist substantially in supporting conservation elements of local land use ordinances and plans.

Local Biodiversity Information

Local governments may decide to commission and fund their own targeted studies to evaluate biodiversity resources, threats, and potential land use choices. There is substantial experience with such studies in the western United

States where endangered species issues have played a major role in land development decisions in recent decades. These represent the high-end, multiyear efforts needed to address multiple endangered species in the context of planning and land use regulation.

Pima County, for example, has been engaged since 1998 in preparing the Sonoran Desert Conservation Plan to integrate habitat conservation with ranch preservation and development scenarios for the county that surrounds Tucson, Arizona. This planning program required the gathering of new, detailed information to document living resources and habitat areas as well as threats posed by varying forms of development. The research was driven by the county's decision to prepare a countywide habitat conservation plan as authorized under the federal ESA. The Act allows persons (including local governments) to obtain U.S. Fish and Wildlife Service (FWS) approval for actions that may affect endangered species—including "incidental takes" of such species—so long as a detailed plan has been prepared that minimizes and mitigates for impacts, and provides for adequately funded conservation measures such that any incidental takes will not "appreciably reduce the likelihood of the survival and recovery of the species in the wild."[18] Pima County's Sonoran Desert Conservation Plan identified areas of conservation importance as "conservation reserves" and also provided support for some federal land conservation decisions within the county, as well as guiding development decisions and land use regulations.[19] Preparation of the plan included substantial local investments in scientific research and studies with upward of 200 papers.[20] The community-based planning team relied heavily on these research studies, and its use of the studies to integrate multiple planning objectives resulted in Pima County's receipt of the Outstanding Planning Award at the American Planning Association's convention in Chicago in 2002. The information base that the county created addresses habitat, ranchland, and cultural resources, among other values.

Communities have also pursued multijurisdictional research. In southern California, for example, integrated conservation planning for multiple species has been used to deal with endangered species issues ranging from the endangered California gnatcatcher to other endangered plants and animals. The research serves as the basis for FWS approvals and for city and county revisions to local comprehensive plans. One of the larger efforts is the Multiple Species Conservation Program involving San Diego County, the city of San Diego, and 10 other incorporated cities. The research program provides support for habitat protection and development decisions.[21]

But local research to support land use planning and decisionmaking is not confined to reliance on statewide data on the one hand, or to ESA-driven research and funding on the other. Many local municipalities, towns, boroughs, townships, and counties have invested in environmental studies that include habitat and biological components. Many of the ordinances discussed in this book are based on local research and judicious reliance on existing resources and expertise. Habitat information is available in many places. For example, local research on amphibians and bird habitat needs by the Metropolitan Conservation Alliance has helped towns in Westchester County, New York, identify where to focus additional development density and where to focus their conservation efforts in order to protect areas of benefit to multiple species.[22]

Local colleges and universities can provide a meaningful resource for conservation information. Not only do professors of biology and ecology frequently have some local projects, but often students can obtain information relatively inexpensively in one or two supervised field seasons. This can support local decisionmaking and supplement state-supplied information by providing either a more detailed focus on particular parcels (river corridors, potential parkland dedications, swamps and bogs, etc.), or by providing at least general data in areas where there is no state information, e.g., local information on the prevalence of invasive exotic plant species, or information on the life-cycle locations of specific local amphibians. This information can be used by local officials, planners, and others to identify potential issues that might otherwise have been missed in preparing a local ordinance and can sometimes enable officials to make some choices that avoid areas of particular concern.

Choosing Land Use Tools

The chapters that follow illustrate how familiar land use tools can be used by local governments to conserve biodiversity resources. The tools are the familiar collection of planning, zoning, subdivision, and police power regulations familiar to all planning professionals. The key difference is that with appropriate biological and ecological information, each of these tools can be used to conserve living organisms and the areas and ecological processes upon which they depend.

Each tool is briefly described. Then its use for biodiversity is explained, relating the tool to the ecological guidelines described in Chapter Two. Then the text identifies *key elements* for effective use of the tool in biodiversity conservation. Planners, attorneys, local government managers, elected officials, and citizen advocates can use the key elements as a checklist to determine whether their ordinances measure up to the requirements of effective conservation planning. Finally, the discussion of each land use tool concludes with the experience of one or more communities that have used it.

The tools are grouped generally into planning and zoning; subdivision and development approval; growth management and infrastructure ordinances; conservation practice ordinances; and publicly owned open space policies. The biological and ecological information should help inform the decisionmaker about what tool to use. Site-specific conservation may be best addressed through land acquisition or through detailed subdivision requirements applicable to designated areas. Broader land conservation goals may be addressed through land use plans, zoning, vegetation ordinances, and other tools.

Although described separately, these tools should be used in combination to meet the conservation guidelines. Effective use of any of these tools begins, as we have seen in this chapter, with identification of reliable information. But the next necessary step is to use the information to develop a plan—the subject of Chapter Four.

Chapter Three Endnotes

1. *See* JOHN R. NOLON, OPEN GROUND: EFFECTIVE LOCAL STRATEGIES FOR PRO-TECTING NATURAL RESOURCES (Envtl. L. Inst. 2003); JOHN R. NOLON, WELL GROUNDED: USING LOCAL LAND USE AUTHORITY TO ACHIEVE SMART GROWTH (Envtl. L. Inst. 2001) [hereinafter NOLON, WELL GROUNDED].

2. PA. STAT. ANN. tit. 53, §10301(a)(6).

3. IAN MCHARG, DESIGN WITH NATURE (Falcon Press 1969).

4. RUTHERFORD H. PLATT, LAND USE AND SOCIETY: GEOGRAPHY, LAW, AND PUBLIC POLICY 318-29 (Island Press 1996).

5. NOLON, WELL GROUNDED, *supra* note 1, at xxiii.

6. 16 U.S.C. §§1531-1544, ELR STAT. ESA §§2-18.

7. SHEILA PECK, PLANNING FOR BIODIVERSITY 115 (1998).

8. *See, e.g.*, AMERICAN MUSEUM OF NATURAL HISTORY ET AL., NEW YORK STATE BIODIVERSITY PROJECT NEEDS ASSESSMENT (2001), *available at* http://www.eli.org/pdf/rr01nybiodiversity.pdf (last visited Dec. 3, 2003).

9. *See* DEFENDERS OF WILDLIFE, INTEGRATING LAND USE PLANNING AND BIODIVERSITY (2003), *available at* http://www.defenders.org/habitat/landuse.pdf (last visited Dec. 3, 2003).

10. NatureServe, *Visit Local Programs*, *at* http://www.natureserve.org/visitLocal/index.jsp (last visited Dec. 3, 2003).

11. CHRISTINA KENNEDY & JESSICA WILKINSON, PLANNING WITH NATURE: BIODIVERSITY INFORMATION IN ACTION (Envtl. L. Inst. 2003), *available at* http://www.elistore.org/reports_detail.asp?ID=10797 (last visited Dec. 3, 2003).

12. National Biological Information Infrastructure, *State Resources*, *at* http://www.nbii.gov/geographic/us/state.html (last visited Dec. 3, 2003). Information and data on national and regional biodiversity trends includes U.S. GEOLOGICAL SURVEY, STATUS AND TRENDS OF THE NATION'S BIOLOGICAL RESOURCES (1998) and BRUCE STEIN ET AL., PRECIOUS HERITAGE: THE STATUS OF BIODIVERSITY IN THE UNITED STATES (Oxford Univ. Press 2000).

13. Pennsylvania Department of Conservation & Natural Resources, *Homepage*, *at* http://www.dcnr.state.pa.us (last visited Dec. 3, 2003).

14. Maryland Department of Natural Resources, *Greenways*, *at* http://www.dnr.state.md.us/greenways (last visited Dec. 3, 2003).

15. GeoPlan, *Florida's Statewide Greenways Planning Project*, *at* http://www.geoplan.ufl.edu/projects/greenways/greenwayindex.html (last visited Dec. 3, 2003).

16. EXECUTIVE OFFICE OF ENVIRONMENTAL AFFAIRS, COMMONWEALTH OF MASSACHU-SETTS, BIOMAP: GUIDING LAND CONSERVATION FOR BIODIVERSITY IN MASSACHU-SETTS (2001).

17. Natural Heritage and Endangered Species Program, Massachusetts Division of Fisheries & Wildlife, *Heritage Introduction*, *at* http://www.state.ma.us/dfwele/dfw/nhesp (last visited Dec. 3, 2003).

18. 16 U.S.C. §1539.

19. Pima County, Arizona, *Sonoran Desert Conservation Plan*, *at* http://www.co.pima.az.us/cmo/sdcp (last visited Dec. 21, 2003).

20. *See generally* DEFENDERS OF WILDLIFE, *supra* note 9, at 46.

21. City of San Diego, *Multiple Species Conservation Program Plan Summary*, *at* http://www.sannet.gov/mscp/plansum.shtml (last visited Dec. 3, 2003).

22. Interview with Dr. Michael Klemens, Wildlife Conservation Society, in Wye Island, Md. (Feb. 28, 2002).

Chapter Four—Planning and Zoning

Planning and zoning mechanisms are well suited to biodiversity conservation. They have the advantages of familiarity and flexibility, and they can be designed to address the conservation guidelines defined in Chapter Two. Planning—especially comprehensive planning—provides the foundation upon which all of the other ordinance tools can rely. Zoning remains the predominant form of local land use regulation for most of the last 80 years. Both of them also define the context within which many of the tools covered in the later chapters operate. This chapter discusses the following planning and zoning measures and their relationship to biodiversity conservation:

- The Comprehensive Plan;
- Zoning Districts;
- Overlay Zones;
- Agricultural Protection Zoning;
- Cluster Zoning;
- Incentive Zoning;
- Performance Zoning; and
- Traditional Neighborhood Development.

The Comprehensive Plan

Description

A "comprehensive plan," or "master plan" (as it is known in some parts of the country) is a written document that defines goals, objectives, and implementation strategies for the future growth and development of the jurisdiction adopting the plan. Comprehensive plans are typically developed by local planning commissions with public input through public hearings. They are formally approved or adopted by the local government's governing body. In some states and in specific types of local jurisdictions (cities, towns, boroughs, townships, counties, villages), comprehensive plans are required, while in others they are optional.[1]

Comprehensive plans define community goals and specify how local governments intend to reach these goals. They guide decisions on adoption and amendment of zoning and subdivision regulations and expenditure of public funds on infrastructure. They influence state and federal siting of facilities such as highways and utility siting of power lines and sewers. They identify and target conservation and acquisition areas, guide capital spending and borrowing choices, and affect private land use decisions. Comprehensive plans do not themselves regulate development activities. Instead, they establish the frame-

31

work within which both regulatory and nonregulatory decisions will be made and ordinances adopted.

Although some state laws require that all local ordinances and regulations conform with the locality's comprehensive plan, others treat comprehensive planning as a valuable but nonbinding device that generally informs the land use regulatory process. Nonetheless, whether binding or advisory, comprehensive planning can provide a blueprint for guiding future development and conservation.

Some state enabling legislation identifies specific required elements for local comprehensive plans. Other state laws simply authorize local planning without identifying required elements. So-called home-rule jurisdictions typically have very broad flexibility as to the contents of their comprehensive plans. The American Planning Association's *Growing Smarter Legislative Guidebook* offers model language for state enabling legislation that suggests that plans include a number of required planning elements, while offering a list of conditionally required or optional elements.[2]

Under current law, every comprehensive plan can include elements that relate to the natural environment—the land and water base on which the community rests. Whether this is based on the simple "land use element" found in virtually all plans or is a more detailed "conservation element" or even "habitat element" found in others, the community is empowered to consider the interaction of its development choices (and its capital expenditures) with the natural environment. This authority, in turn, can support consideration of biodiversity as part of the plan. A study by the Environmental Law Institute and the Center for Wildlife Law identifies language in the planning enabling statutes of every state that can be used to support local biodiversity planning in the context of comprehensive plans.[3]

Comprehensive planning is an important phase of land use regulation and planning. Integration of biodiversity conservation into a land use plan provides a basis for use of all of the other tools discussed in this book. In addition, the plan can be structured to anticipate the future collection and receipt of information on biological resources so that even where detailed information is currently lacking future information can be used to help shape the community's growth and quality of life decisions. The plan sets forth the policies for action by the local government.

Use for Biodiversity

Comprehensive planning can address all of the conservation guidelines outlined in Chapter Two. A comprehensive plan is an ideal vehicle in which to identify large contiguous areas of habitat and the connections between them. It can define a community goal of conserving the ecological integrity of such areas, whatever their projected development status. A plan is also helpful in establishing a commitment to identify and protect rare landscape elements, sensitive areas, and species. The comprehensive plan can and should identify natural resources that are subject to depletion through incompatible land uses.

Comprehensive planning that takes biodiversity into account could, for example, be highly useful in a fast growing county where planning authority is vested in the county government. Suppose that rapid development has begun to lead—as it so often does—to problems with traffic congestion, loss of traditional agricultural uses, and conflict with endangered species habitat. Such factors could lead county officials to undertake preparation of a new or amended comprehensive plan that contains natural resources and habitat elements. If the planners took ecological guidelines into account, the plan could include provisions for:

- a county inventory of living resources and habitat types and locations;
- identification of opportunities for retaining agricultural lands and a goal of conserving biodiversity on multiple use and resource lands;
- designation of denser development areas that avoid vulnerable habitats, areas of biodiversity richness or uniqueness, and habitat cores and corridors;
- development guidelines that minimize and mitigate for impacts of authorized development activities;
- a capital improvement plan that addresses habitat and conservation impacts, including provision for investments in "green infrastructure" like open space, and designated goals for mitigation of capital infrastructure impacts; and
- elements supporting a habitat conservation plan if needed to address federal Endangered Species Act concerns.

Comprehensive planning that includes biodiversity conservation can also be used in small municipalities where the municipal government regulates land use. Consider a case in which a semi-rural township currently lacks a plan but has a zoning ordinance that zones most of the land for residential development at a uniform density of one dwelling unit per acre. The county's master plan (which is advisory only) designates the township as low density residential and does not identify any resources of county significance in the township. Without further action, the township could be subdivided into parcels that make it difficult to provide public services and that have no value for biodiversity, forestry, agriculture, or tourism. In such an instance, a new township master plan could provide for an inventory of natural resources, identify habitat cores and corridors, and define the basis for potential zoning for cluster development or areas of greater density intended to protect farm and forest land as well as biological resources. In preparing a plan, it will be particularly important for the township planning board to seek information outside the township boundary and to seek some level of compatibility in planning that recognizes the conditions of habitat and development restrictions in adjacent jurisdictions.[4]

Key Biodiversity Elements

The comprehensive plan should have the following key elements.

1. The comprehensive plan should explicitly recognize the larger ecological region within which the plan operates. If the plan is being prepared in a jurisdiction where there is an existing statewide ecological mapping program—such as Massachusetts's BioMap, Florida's Greenways System, or the Maryland Green Infrastructure program—the connections can be readily made. However, even absent such specific state planning information, local jurisdictions can draw upon state natural heritage programs for data on rare and threatened ecosystems, state wildlife and natural resources programs for habitat and natural area data and plans, and on nonprofit organizations for regional ecological data—such as The Nature Conservancy's "ecoregional plans" now being prepared to cover the entire nation.[5] The comprehensive plan should be clear about how decisions about natural areas and biodiversity within the local jurisdiction are expected to contribute to, or relate to, the larger landscape function.

2. The plan should rely upon available data and scientific information concerning species and habitat presence, needs, stressors, and benefits. Where little information is initially available, the plan may specify how the local government will go about obtaining the information over time.

3. The plan should provide for *core areas* where development activities will be most strictly limited (or where land or easement acquisitions should be targeted), as well as for *supporting landscapes* that provide connections between and among core areas.[6]

4. The plan should incorporate residents' identification of key environmental values and of local land and water areas that contribute to quality of life. The planning body or staff can hold meetings and focused discussions of living resources and habitat issues during plan development in order to assure that the conservation elements reflect public input and understanding. While public input of this sort is not a substitute for good scientific information on habitat and conservation needs, it can inform governmental choices about land uses in specific areas of concern that have been identified through scientific analysis. Attention to community preferences can also help develop support for environmentally oriented elements in the comprehensive plan by linking them with social goals.

5. The plan should provide for some conservation measures that can apply jurisdictionwide. Plans should not simply designate critical or sensitive areas but should also identify potential measures that may apply to the broader matrix of lands within which these exist. These measures may include, for example, plans for residents' or government's use of native plant species, identifying the need for water use and conservation goals, measures related to tree canopy, measures for stormwater management using landscape tools, and broad require-

ments for mitigation of unavoidable environmental impairments. Biodiversity conservation includes some factors that apply across the landscape, and including the entire community in actions that have environmental value helps to build support for the more specific plans that deal with designated areas.

6. The plan should address governmental infrastructure and open space investments and identify how to integrate the conservation guidelines into these expenditures of public funds.

7. Last, the plan should provide for accountability measures. It must define specific conservation objectives in terms that can enable the local government and citizens to know whether the plan is achieving its objectives. Vague objectives produce no accountability and few results.

Comprehensive Plan—Hopewell Township, New Jersey

In 2002, Hopewell Township, New Jersey, a suburbanizing township not far from Princeton, adopted a newly revised master plan.[7] The plan identifies a township goal to retain large contiguous tracts of farmland and other open space. It includes resource conservation initiatives to protect lands that contain natural systems that are critical to the ecological function of the area. The new plan includes as an additional objective: "To protect biological diversity through the maintenance of large contiguous tracts and corridors of recreation, forest, flood plain and other open space lands."[8]

A conservation plan element outlines the township's strategies for meeting this and the other conservation goals of the plan. In conjunction with the land use plan element, the conservation element addresses the location, scale, and intensity of new development and strategies to manage resources.[9] Among other goals, the conservation plan seeks to limit the impacts of development, to retain natural terrain and landscape features, and to support the restoration of degraded natural systems. It is designed to shape the development permitted by the land use plan to preserve and protect the township's natural resources. It involves agencies in addition to the planning board in the effort to protect resources.[10] The new biodiversity language also provides further support for the township's existing "valley resource conservation district" and "mountain resource conservation district," which comprise over 75% of the township and in which tools like minimum lot sizes, clustering, and lot averaging are used to maintain open space.

A forest resources and native vegetation component of the conservation plan element identifies approaches to conserve, protect, and improve the quality of forest resources within the township. The plan recommends that the township establish performance standards that limit the extent of forest removal in connection with various land development activities and that conservation priority be given to specific wooded areas, such as unique forest types, habitats critical for endangered and threatened species, wetlands, stream corridors, and steep slopes.[11] The forest resources component also recommends the development of performance standards that encourage the preservation of habitat areas that are as large and circular as possible and connected by wildlife corridors large enough to maintain interior habitat conditions.[12] This component of the plan was designed in accordance with the recommendations of a study of the remaining forest stands in the township. The study evaluated and prioritized protection areas and helped lead to the drafting of a woodlands protection ordinance, which has not yet been adopted.[13]

The conservation plan element includes a component on threatened and endangered plant and animal species, which recommends that the township conduct an ongoing inventory of threatened, endangered, and declining species, and that it prohibit development that would adversely impact these species. These species are identified through the New Jersey state natural heritage database. A number of groups are participating in inventorying species in the township.[14] The plan also recommends that critical habitats be mapped and preserved, either through open space acquisition or the development review process. In addition, the plan suggests that the township preserve nodes of biodiversity wherever they occur and reduce residential density and impervious surfaces in critical habitat areas. The plan calls for the use of land use tools, including zoning and regulation to "maximize the conservation of substantial masses of critical habitat areas by limiting the aerial extent of development and promoting conservation techniques targeted to these resources."[15]

The master plan guides the township's goal to acquire and preserve open space as well as to implement an open space planning incentive program and woodland and stream corridor protection ordinances. The conservation element of the master plan is important in establishing the basis for implementation strategies that encourage the acquisition and preservation of open space that is identified as having value for biodiversity. The township currently dedicates a tax of $.03 per $100 of assessed property value to support bonds used for the acquisition of open space, sometimes combining this funding with state Green Acres funding.

Comprehensive Plan—Albemarle County, Virginia

Counties are required to prepare comprehensive plans under Virginia law. Albemarle County's comprehensive plan has been amended several times to deal with the effects of rapid population growth and sprawl in the area surrounding Charlottesville. Plan amendments have promoted the concentration of development in designated development areas and maintaining rural areas as productive farm or forest land. The plan contains a chapter on natural resources, which provides guidelines on open space and open space planning, including the planning of greenways, and lists a number of natural resources slated for further action. In 1999, the county added a new element to this portion of its comprehensive plan in order to include biodiversity among the goals to be pursued in land use management and regulation.[16]

The new Biological Resources and Biodiversity plan element established a county planning goal to "recognize the importance of protecting biological diversity in both the Rural Area and the Development Areas for the ecological, aesthetic, ethical, and economic benefits to the community."[17] The new plan element describes the importance of species diversity, genetic diversity, and ecosystem diversity and connects them to community well-being. It includes a list of native species and ecological communities in Albemarle County identified by the state's natural heritage program, and it identifies habitat destruction and fragmentation (especially forest loss) as the major causes for the reduction of biodiversity in the county. The plan identifies specific activities within the county that contribute to fragmented habitat, including new subdivisions in woodlands, power line locations, and roads, among others.[18]

Albemarle County's Biological Resources and Biodiversity plan element offers a clearly reproducible, incremental way for a community to address biodiversity in the absence of a detailed inventory and before committing to a specific regulatory or other approach. The plan element defines a sequence of actions in which each step leads to the next. This prevents this plan element from simply becoming a high-flown statement of intent that does not lead to action. Specifically, the plan prescribes the commencement and implementation of a biodiversity program and defines three discrete objectives with defined implementation measures.

The first program objective is to increase community awareness of the value of biodiversity and of methods to protect biological resources. The implementation measure prescribed in the plan calls for the county to develop and disseminate educational and technical materials to residents and businesses. Examples of messages to landowners outlined in the plan include information on minimizing lawn areas; putting up nesting boxes; keeping livestock out of streams; maintaining large contiguous patches of woods, meadows, wetlands, and streams; and avoiding the introduction of exotic and non-native plants.

The second defined objective is the completion of a Biological Resources Inventory. The plan calls for the county to conduct an inventory in order to develop systematic knowledge about the types and distribution of biological resources in the county. In order to assure that the inventory is responsive to citizen needs and that it does not become a mere planning staff function that may fall through the cracks in light of other duties, the plan requires the establishment of a citizen advisory committee "to oversee the development of a Biological Resources Inventory and its integration into the planning process."[19] The plan recommends using the county's geographic information system and existing state and local databases and aerial and satellite images for preliminary information, as well as reliance on citizens, university resources, and local consulting foresters. The plan defines the responsibilities of the advisory committee in detail: developing educational materials; developing methods and overseeing the inventory; soliciting cooperation from neighboring counties for a regional inventory; and evaluating implementation options and developing cost estimates. Most important for the stepwise approach, the advisory committee has two publicly accountable duties: (1) assisting county planning staff in developing an action plan that specifies detailed steps for achieving protection of biodiversity as outlined in the comprehensive plan; *and* (2) reporting regularly to the county Board of Supervisors on the status of biodiversity and the planning program.

The third objective is the action plan itself. Under the comprehensive plan, the action plan must address: how the information obtained from the Biological Resources Inventory will be incorporated into land use decisions by the county; creating procedures for the establishment and maintenance of an ongoing biological resources database; the establishment of educational programs; identification of voluntary measures that could be taken to protect areas identified as comprising significant biological resources (including conservation easements and creation of tax incentive districts); and identification of the need for staff or training resources to carry out the action plan.[20]

In carrying out this sequence, the county created a Biodiversity Workgroup to serve as a precursor to the advisory committee. The workgroup, composed of naturalists and scientists, is building the county's biological inventory. This inventory focuses on creating a list of species of concern, identifying the importance of connected landscapes and larger ecological regions, identifying important sites, and getting community input. At the end of the 18-month process, the workgroup will submit a lengthy report with the biological information and suggestions for future policies. Then the standing advisory committee will be appointed by the board. The committee will continue the inventory process, prepare the action plan, and advise the Board of Supervisors on what policies to implement.[21]

The Albemarle County approach recognizes the possibility of planning for biodiversity through a set of incremental processes. It represents a strong alternative to declining to address biodiversity until a substantial amount of information is already in hand.

Zoning Districts

Description

Zoning ordinances divide a community into districts and prescribe the land uses and intensity of development allowed in each district. By establishing use districts—such as commercial, residential, industrial, mixed use, agricultural, or conservation districts—zoning plays a key role in directing growth and controlling development in the community. The zoning ordinance prescribes which specific uses are authorized, which are conditionally authorized, and which are prohibited in each district. Zoning districts often also address density, setback requirements, design standards, and other features affecting the form of development as well as its location. The zoning map shows the location of the districts within the local government's geographical jurisdiction. Where there is a comprehensive plan, the zoning implements the policies defined in the plan. (Most, but not all, zoning is pursuant to a comprehensive plan. Some states authorize zoning by some municipal entities independent of a separate planning requirement. In these municipalities, many of the key elements and choices discussed above under comprehensive planning will need to be addressed in the first instance in the zoning ordinance.)

Use for Biodiversity

Through their restrictions on uses, density, and design, zoning ordinances play a critical role in biodiversity conservation. For example, a zoning ordinance can prevent traffic-intensive or people-intensive activities from occurring close to prime habitat areas, migration corridors, or wildlife reproduction areas.[22]

For example, consider a county that is currently developing at a modest rate. A recent build-out analysis shows that the county is seriously overzoned for commercial development and that it is unlikely to attract this amount of development. Moreover, the overzoning increases the likelihood that when commercial development occurs it will be in dispersed, haphazard, disconnected areas across the county. Simply changing more of the zoning to residential is not likely to be that helpful either, as public facilities have not been planned to handle population increases. For several years the county has simply been rezoning on demand whenever a sizable residential or commercial development proposal came before it. Such a situation calls out for an overhaul of the zoning ordinance. The comprehensive plan, revised some years ago, identified a "foothills region" within the county as an area for special attention but nothing much was done with this provision at the time. An environmental advisory commission assisting the planning board has more recently identified a number of important habitat features of the foothills area—including migration corridors for mammals, a number of springs (regarded primarily as a hazard or water management problem by developers), and two colonies of wild native orchids that are regionally rare but not listed as threatened or endangered. It is evidently time to consider a revision of the zoning ordinance and map. It would be possible to adopt specific zoning districts for the foothills areas and for other portions of the county, and to specify particular uses, mixtures of uses, and densities to be allowed in these areas consistent with the biology and the underlying lands and waters. A zoning ordinance could set specific uses and densities to protect key areas and could concentrate certain kinds of development in other places.

In Ohio's Rootstown Township in Portage County, the governing body designated an "Open Space Conservation District" in order to "protect the ecologic balance of an area to conserve natural resources" including a river valley and tracts of forest land. The district, which established a five-acre minimum lot size in a part of the township that was dominated by wetlands, was upheld as a proper zoning ordinance.[23] While the wetland and forest concerns led Rootstown to adopt large-lot zoning, there are many other approaches that can be used such as mandatory clustering, design requirements, and others. Large-lot zoning is often familiar to local officials and planners but can usually be improved upon. Note that large-lot zoning is often incompatible with biodiversity conservation—it violates numerous conservation guidelines including impairing large unfragmented habitats. Spreading development out across the landscape can also lead to more roads and driveways, as well as become a vehicle for introduction of exotic species. And of course large-lot zoning can also be challengeable as exclusionary zoning where it is an excuse to exclude lower income homeowners. Sometimes a zoning ordinance can use a combination of density and clustering requirements to accomplish a conservation objective.

In addition to the use and density provisions of the zoning ordinance, an ordinance may also prescribe specific procedures to protect biodiversity. The town of Beverly Shores, Indiana, along the shores of Lake Michigan, adopted a zoning ordinance to restrict developments that would affect the local dune system. The entire town is in the dunes area. Specifically, the ordinance provided that applicants for building permits must employ "planning and design to fit the topography, soils, geology, hydrology and other conditions existing on the proposed site" and orient the planning and design to the site "so that grading and other site preparation is kept to an absolute minimum." The ordinance also required that development of the site be timed so that "construction can be completed within one construction season in order that areas are not left bare and exposed during the winter-spring period." The ordinance further required the developer to provide "[l]andscaping of areas around the proposed structure in a manner which blends into the natural topography [and] minimum disruption of existing plant or ground cover." The ordinance was upheld the Indiana Supreme Court as a proper exercise of the town's power to plan and zone for the protection of the "general welfare."[24]

Key Biodiversity Elements

The zoning ordinance should include the following key elements.

1. The zoning ordinance should reference explicit goals contained in the comprehensive plan. A sound zoning ordinance should implement articulated biodiversity goals, open space goals, water quality and habitat goals, and similar natural resources goals.

2. The ordinance should define the basis for development intensity and location with rational reference to the biological needs of the resources to be protected. Requirements for clustering, density, setbacks, and similar restrictions should be based on findings regarding habitat corridors, habitat patch size, biological life-cycle requirements, buffer requirements, and similar findings. Linkage to the science will lead to better ordinance drafting for effectiveness and will avoid over-regulation. Articulation of specific scientific conservation findings in the ordinance will also help guide local decisionmakers as they consider future site-specific decisions about whether specific variances or conditional uses are consistent with the underlying goals of the zoning ordinance.

3. The zoning ordinance and map should be designed to conserve contiguous lands (avoiding fragmentation), maintain connections among habitat parcels, protect rare and sensitive species, conserve waterways and riparian corridors, and address mitigation issues.

4. The drafter of the ordinance should determine whether to create specific separate zoning districts (specifying uses, density, intensity consistent with the particular biodiversity goal for the district), or whether to rely on overlay zones to address biodiversity concerns (see section on overlay zones, below). In general, an overlay zone may be appropriate where much of the area has already been built out or where a specific biodiversity conservation concern cuts across numerous use districts. Otherwise, designing a specific zoning district may be optimal.

5. Consider defining potentially problematic land uses as "conditional uses" in the zones where conservation is important. This approach can enable the local government to evaluate in specific cases whether the use can be designed in a way that adequately protects wildlife migration routes, vegetation, streamflow, and other areas of concern such as pollution prevention.

Zoning Districts—Town of Washington, New York

Washington is a rural town north of Poughkeepsie. It surrounds the separate incorporated village of Millbrook. Throughout the 1970s and 1980s, the town was zoned entirely for residential development at 1-acre, 2-acre, 5-acre, and 10-acre minimum lot sizes, with a small amount of land zoned for strip commercial and industrial development. This zoning scheme began to result in fragmented, scattered development, adversely affecting the natural landscape. In 1989, the town adopted a new zoning ordinance that rezoned much of the undeveloped land at a density (not lot size) of 10 acres per dwelling unit. The actual lot size may be quite a bit smaller (using cluster development techniques),[25] but the density limit is maintained across the lots. This makes it possible to provide for larger areas of habitat, natural lands, stream corridors, and forest land while avoiding cookie-cutter development patterns and too-small lot sizes. Under the ordinance, mandatory clustering may be required for developments affecting contiguous stretches of farmland, forests, and wetlands. The town also makes use of overlay zones and zoning incentives to encourage protection of larger contiguous tracts of land and to encourage development at even less than the allowable density. In collaboration with the village of Millbrook, the town eliminated its strip commercial zones. This benefitted the town by preventing misuse of rural highways and maintaining its rural character, while also benefitting the village of Millbrook, which was enabled to retain businesses and commercial investment. The ordinance was developed in collaboration with the Dutchess Land Conservancy.[26]

Zoning and Planning for Annexation—City of Boise, Idaho

Boise adopted a comprehensive plan in 1997, with an emphasis on growth management and avoiding sprawl. Parts of the plan emphasize new urbanism and traditional neighborhood design. The plan also includes a network of stream corridors and greenways, open space lands, and a provision for the protection of foothills areas, which is further covered by a separate foothills development plan.[27]

The comprehensive plan and implementing ordinances require that all development in this area (which includes anticipated annexation and rezoning areas) must be by planned (unit) development, thus giving the city greater control over the orderly development of this regionally sensitive area. The ordinance provides for clustering of development and set-aside of open spaces with priorities for slopes, riparian areas, and preservation of areas of "highest wildlife habitat value and contiguous wildlife migration corridors."[28]

Interestingly, Boise established the basis for its anticipated zoning and development requirements for these areas in advance of annexation. "Upon annexation, the buildable areas of the [planned development (PD)] shall be zoned 1-A 'Single-Family Residential' with the density and design further controlled by the provisions of this ordinance. Slope protection and preserved open space areas shall be zoned A 'Open.'"[29] Under the city's zoning ordinance, zoning classification district A—Open Space Land—authorizes single family residential development, public park, or golf course uses. Schools, private recreation or amusement facilities, planned unit development, golf course clubhouses less than 300 feet from residences, sand and gravel operations, churches, cemeteries, kennels, animal hospitals, aircraft landing fields, government buildings, broadcasting towers, agriculture, and child care facilities are identified as conditional uses that may be authorized.[30] In the foothills area, specific additional provisions will apply under the planned unit development standards to ensure the protection and conservation of key habitat and ecological resources.

Overlay Zones

Description

Overlay zones are specially created districts in which new land use provisions apply in addition to those contained in the underlying zoning ordinance. Overlay zones therefore supplement the underlying zoning standards with additional requirements. Overlay zoning can be visualized as a paintbrush that superimposes additional rules for the areas within its brushstroke. Areas within the brushstroke are simultaneously subject to both the underlying and overlay zoning requirements. Outside the brushstroke, only the underlying zoning requirements apply. Overlay zoning is an important device because it enables local governments to impose additional regulations on specific areas without amending the basic zoning ordinance defining uses and development intensity for the district or districts covered.

Overlay zones can vary in size, from occupying a portion of an existing zoning district to spreading across several zoning districts. Overlay zoning is often used where the existing zoning law adequately regulates the district or districts generally but additional provisions are necessary to achieve particular land use objectives in the specified area. For example, overlay zones may be used to protect a particular natural resource such as a wetland, watershed, or wildlife migration corridor. Overlay zoning is particularly useful when areas in need of protection go across multiple zones, as it eliminates the need to tailor revised regulations for each zoning district covered.

Overlay zoning is a flexible, multipurpose tool used to superimpose rules that can be either more restrictive or permissive than the underlying zoning ordinance. To illustrate, a community could create an overlay zone with more restrictive, conservation-oriented rules such as steep slope protection regulations, setback provisions, or tree-protection measures in order to protect environmentally sensitive or critical areas. Moreover, a community could couple this conservation overlay with a separate development overlay zone with more permissive rules, such as tax breaks for redevelopment or higher density allowances, thus providing incentives to guide development towards these less sensitive areas. Overlay zoning can be used in conjunction with more specific land use regulations to meet the conservation and development goals of the community.

Use for Biodiversity

Overlay zones are extremely useful in protecting rare landscape elements and sensitive areas, such as bogs, prairies, ridge tops, dunes, wetlands, springs, and cave areas. *See* Figure 3. They are also helpful in assuring the identification and maintenance of contiguous habitat areas that cut across a number of use districts.

Figure 3: Overlay Zone

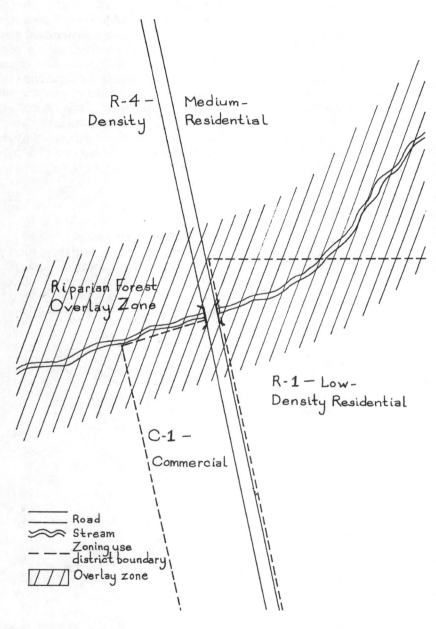

R-4 – Medium-Density Residential

Riparian Forest Overlay Zone

R-1 – Low-Density Residential

C-1 – Commercial

Road
Stream
Zoning use district boundary
Overlay zone

Drawing by Kathryn Hubler

For example, consider a town that is currently zoned for various densities of residential development over its entire area. Recently, a regional study has revealed that portions of the town contain a complex of wetland and vernal pools that are regionally important for migratory bird stopovers and for local populations of common amphibians. The town is likely to experience continued residential development. An overlay district could be a strong approach that can assure the functions and viability of the identified area by imposing additional conditions and restrictions on development within the area and adjacent to it. The overlay can accommodate various forms and densities of development, but should require additional studies, mitigation measures, reconfiguration of hardened infrastructure, changes in lot coverage, design requirements, and other measures to protect the resources of concern. Thus, while residential development may still be authorized within the overlay zone, the resulting homes may be placed away from the vernal pools, driveways may be shorter, dwelling footprints may be reduced, accessory buildings may be prohibited, outside lighting may be limited or restricted to certain types, and dedications of easements covering the wetlands may be required.

Key Biodiversity Elements

The overlay ordinance should have the following key elements for biodiversity.

1. The ordinance should clearly define the purpose and need for the overlay. Preferably this should be done with reference to the comprehensive plan as well as to public health, safety, and welfare concerns. If there is an explicit biodiversity or natural resource conservation goal in the plan, it too should be referenced. The connection between the overlay and community goals is a key basis for a sound overlay ordinance. If the comprehensive plan has only general language, the ordinance drafter should make explicit the connection of the overlay ordinance to those goals that are articulated, as well as to any state goals and requirements that may support the overlay ordinance.

2. The ordinance should assure that habitat core areas and connections are protected by identifying them explicitly on the zoning map.

3. The ordinance should specify clear and simple requirements. If the ordinance spells out precisely what needs to be done by landowners within the overlay zone, compliance becomes easier to obtain and enforcement is possible. Vague overlay provisions do not improve community support for the ordinance. They also can needlessly consume local government staff time and developer time and resources. In achieving sufficient specificity in the ordinance, different requirements might be applied to core areas than to corridors, for example.

4. Make sure that the overlay provisions are biologically significant. An overlay that imposes conditions that do not accomplish the desired objective is not worth having.

5. Consider limitations on linear features that may fragment habitat (roads, pipelines, driveways, electric and utility lines), and consider requiring co-location of such features to minimize fragmentation.

6. Consider defining mitigation measures that might apply to activities or uses within the overlay zone that cause unavoidable losses or impairments.

7. Connect the overlay district to adjacent habitat areas where this will serve the biodiversity conservation objectives—even if the adjacent area is in another jurisdiction. Biodiversity is not typically congruent with municipal (or even county) boundaries. Whenever possible, the overlay should explicitly identify its relationship to land and water and biodiversity resources on the greater landscape even though the local government cannot regulate activities on extraterritorial lands. Making this connection helps make it possible for other local governments, state entities, and private conservation efforts to take consistent actions in the future, and further reinforces the scientific basis for the overlay.

Overlay Zone—Falmouth, Massachusetts

The town of Falmouth, Massachusetts, adopted a Wildlife Corridor Protection Bylaw designating an overlay zone.[31] Town planners designed the bylaw "to establish and protect permanent and contiguous corridors and special areas for the feeding, breeding[,] and normal home range movement of wildlife through the defined habitat areas."[32] The bylaw was adopted by a vote of the town meeting in 1988 following public hearings held by the planning board. The bylaw implements part of a strategy to serve natural resource goals. These goals have been most recently set forth in the local comprehensive plan adopted by the town meeting in 1998.[33]

The wildlife corridors defined in the overlay bylaw are based on white tail deer migration trails and habitat data compiled by the Natural Resources Department. At the time of the adoption of the bylaw, the white tail deer was considered an indicator species for the health of the area environment. The overlay zones cover the white tail deer migration pattern between Camp Edwards/Otis Air Force Base to Naushon Island off Woods Hole—providing a connection between two "core" areas. Because of the migration patterns, it was determined that an overlay zone was more appropriate than a townwide bylaw.

The overlay bylaw requires that subdivisions that total more than 10 acres in the town's AGA, AGB, RA, PU, and RB zones and more than 20 acres in the AGAA and RAA zones apply for a special permit, and further provides that the planning board may require a cluster-type subdivision as a condition of such permit. (These categories include most of the zoning district types in which new development is possible). Landowners must establish contiguous corridors with a minimum 300-foot width across the land parcel and connecting to adjacent parcels and corridors. Fencing and other structural barriers are prohibited within the corridors. The bylaw also specifies that indigenous vegetation shall be encouraged or enhanced by the project.

The single species focus of the corridor design does not protect the full range of biodiversity in the town. However, the designation of substantial upland connected corridors between two areas with substantial open space provides a means to improve potential biological diversity benefits on a landscape basis. The bylaw also provides for an annual report by the Natural Resources Department evaluating the corridors and open space and any needs for changes in vegetation management. This aspect of the bylaw creates the basis for continuing adaptive management and evaluation of appropriate amendments if needed.

Agricultural Protection Zoning

Description

Development pressure often leads to the conversion of agricultural land to developed uses, thus destroying and fragmenting wildlife habitat formerly found around farming operations. In order to protect these areas, communities can adopt some variant of agricultural protection zoning. Agricultural protection zoning serves the dual function of maintaining parcels of land that are large enough to sustain economically viable agricultural use while also assuring that the lands are not converted to developed uses that are permanently incompatible with biodiversity conservation.

Agricultural protection zoning designates an area as an agricultural district subject to specific regulation under the zoning laws. Typically, in such zones agricultural uses are permitted as-of-right, while non-farm uses are either prohibited or allowed subject to certain conditions. This use restriction may be combined with other restrictions such as prohibitions on the subdivision of agricultural land or requirements that subdivisions result in parcels that are quite large. Related techniques include large minimum lot sizes, cluster development or conservation development requirements, limits on the number of building permits authorized for the zone, and regulations confining buildable areas within the zone to poorer soils or smaller tracts.

A common approach limits subdivision of agricultural tracts so that subdivisions are allowed only if each resulting tract will contain 100 or more acres; such ordinances sometimes also provide for development of 1 additional dwelling on the original parcel in order to allow family members to remain on the farm in accordance with historical practices in much of the United States. Another allows subdivision but limits development to a number of small lots, e.g., less than one acre, while preserving the remaining tract of land for agriculture. Fixed area-based agricultural zoning establishes a specific number of dwellings per number of acres in the original tract—such as 1 dwelling per 25 acres. However, the dwellings must be constructed on relatively small building lots, leaving the remaining parcel intact for agriculture. Sliding scale agricultural zoning is a variation on this technique that allows higher density development on smaller tracts than on large tracts in order to preserve the larger tracts for agriculture. Under this approach, a farm parcel of 100 acres might be allowed to support a development of 5 residential dwelling units (clustered on small parcels, with the remainder reserved for agriculture), while a farm parcel of 250 acres might be allowed to support a development of 9 dwelling units (with similar restrictions).[34]

Historically, large-lot requirements have been used to protect agricultural areas from development by limiting development density and therefore making nonagricultural uses less attractive. However, large-lot zoning by itself is often incompatible with biodiversity conservation and does not necessarily support the continuation of farming. Rather, large-lot zoning (particularly where it relies on lots of 5-20 acres rather than those viable for farming) often hastens the spread of sprawl development by scattering housing even more diffusely across the rural landscape. Large-lot zoning has been largely discredited as a farmland protection technique, except where it is used in conjunction with other restrictions on non-farm uses that adequately preserve land in agricultural use.

Use for Biodiversity

Agricultural zoning can serve biodiversity conservation objectives by effectively providing for large habitat areas (preventing fragmentation), by allowing for at least some continuation of natural patterns of disturbance (wind, rain, sometimes fire), providing connections among habitat areas, and avoiding depleting land uses. Agriculture is not always compatible with biodiversity—intensive row-crop agriculture, for example, may not support biodiversity (particularly where the land is cropped fence-row to fence-row and substantial chemical inputs are used). But the rural landscape in general provides opportunities to support biodiversity, and where the land is managed to include a matrix of vegetation and variety of habitats, can be very important in biodiversity conservation.

Agricultural zoning might be considered, for example, in a farming community that is beginning to experience second home and retirement home development. Under current subdivision and zoning regulations, 20-acre parcels are being created and developed for these purposes, thus putting pressure on continued farming and on the connectivity of habitat. The local government could adopt a zoning ordinance that provides for minimum 50-acre parcels but allows cluster development on split-off one-acre or one-half acre parcels based on a density calculation so that the farmers do not lose any of the density they currently are allowed. Thus, rather than subdividing into 10 20-acre "farmettes" by right under existing zoning or subdivision regulations, the owner of a 200-acre farm wishing to subdivide would be allowed by the ordinance to subdivide into 10 adjacent 1-acre parcels, with 190 acres conserved for agricultural use. Alternatively, the owner could subdivide into 4 50-acre parcels, meeting the new minimum requirement for the agricultural zoning district. This would provide parcels large enough to sustain farming and biodiversity benefits.

The agricultural use language of the ordinance should be written to allow conservation uses on the agricultural parcel—so that such lands could be woodland, wildlife areas, horticultural areas, and other uses compatible with conservation goals.

Key Biodiversity Elements

The agricultural zoning ordinance should contain the following key elements.

1. The ordinance drafters should make sure that the residual agricultural lots are big enough to sustain farming and the desired ecological purposes. A common failing of agricultural zoning results in the creation of "farmettes" or mini-estates that cannot support farming economically, while contributing to fragmentation of the landscape and habitats by spreading sprawl development across a larger area.

2. The ordinance should require clustering and/or specify small lots for the developable parcels. Maximum lot size limitations are a method for doing this. (See section on cluster zoning, below).

3. The ordinance should include a requirement to plan for connection with open space uses on adjacent lands. The ordinance should not result in an individually preserved farmstead (or series of disconnected farmsteads) each surrounded by cul-de-sac suburban tract housing, manicured corporate campuses, or industrial parks. The conserved areas should link to one another if possible.

4. Be sure to allow compatible nonagricultural uses of the residual parcel—open space, forestry, horticulture, wildlife habitat, biodiversity conservation—but not intensive uses, extensive impervious surfaces, or development. Possibly, low-intensity, home-based businesses could also be authorized in order to assist in maintaining the economic viability of those engaged in farming and conservation uses.

Agricultural Protection Zoning—Berks County, Pennsylvania

Berks County, in eastern Pennsylvania, contains large amounts of agricultural and rural land. Farming has continuously occupied 70 to 90% of the land in the county's rural townships since settlement in the late 1600s. About 40% of the land countywide is still devoted to agriculture.[35]

In Pennsylvania, authority for municipal and county zoning comes from the Municipalities Planning Code, which authorizes zoning for the "protection and promotion of natural resources and agricultural land and activities."[36] The commonwealth of Pennsylvania also has a Farmland Protection Program, established by law in1988, which provides for acquisition of agricultural conservation easements by the state or counties.[37]

Zoning in Pennsylvania is carried out by municipal governments, although local municipalities may agree to accept county zoning. By 1997, 12 Berks County municipalities had adopted agricultural zoning ordinances, covering over 58,000 acres.[38] Spurred by the county's Agricultural Zoning Incentive

Program, in which the county paid all administrative costs associated with municipalities' amending their zoning ordinances to incorporate effective agricultural zoning, this trend continued.[39] Currently, approximately 100,000 acres are covered by municipal agricultural zoning ordinances out of approximately 200,000 acres in farming use countywide.

Bethel Township adopted the county's standard agricultural zoning ordinance in 2000. The intent of the ordinance is to "promote agricultural land uses and activities and other uses and activities which act in direct support of agriculture" in order to maintain agriculture as an ongoing economic activity.[40] The ordinance does this by limiting nonagricultural use of farm lands within the zone. It differentiates agricultural land use and activities from incompatible residential, commercial, and industrial development.

The ordinance regulates subdivision for nonagricultural uses. It defines a farm parcel as a Parent Tract, and specifically limits residential development by specifying that "a second and all subsequent single-family detached dwellings to be erected upon the Parent Tract [or subdivided from the tract] shall be permitted only by special exception."[41] These special exceptions are subject to a sliding scale of acreage, which allows 1 additional dwelling on a tract of 1-20 acres, 2 on a tract of 20-50 acres, 3 on a tract of 50-100 acres, 4 on a tract of 100-200 acres, 5 on a tract of 200-300 acres, and 6 on a tract of 300 acres or greater.[42] Thus, the ordinance conserves larger farm tracts, reducing density as the size of the original parent tract increases. The ordinance also requires that any proposed nonagricultural uses (including dwelling units) must be clustered in order to preserve the greatest extent of productive and valuable farmland. And it requires that residential development must be placed on the least productive soils of the parent tract.[43]

Bethel Township's Agricultural Preservation District contains other provisions that have the potential to protect biodiversity and reduce human impact on natural resources. The ordinance lists a number of "uses permitted by right" in the Agricultural Preservation District. These include "woodland or game preserve, wildlife sanctuary or similar conservation use."[44] While their primary intent is not natural habitat or biodiversity protection, the Berks County townships' agricultural protection ordinances contain provisions that lead to the protection of important natural lands. In addition to the primary effect of reducing commercial and residential development and preserving large tracts capable of supporting farming, many Berks County ordinances provide for such features as natural buffer zones and open space.

The benefits of farmland preservation in Berks County extend beyond the individual parcels conserved. The nationally known Hawk Mountain Sanctuary, a well-known primary raptor habitat, is on the western edge of the county, and the farmland provides a hunting area for these birds, thus providing a biodiversity benefit that redounds to the benefit of the entire area—indeed the entire region.

Cluster Zoning

Description

Cluster zoning provides the opportunity or requirement for developers to construct buildings in clusters while remaining within the constraints of overall average density restrictions. Under cluster zoning, maximum densities are calculated for the overall development area but the construction is limited to smaller parcels that are typically adjacent to one another. This concentrates development on a smaller area of the overall tract while allowing (or requiring) developers to set aside larger areas of open space.

For example, if a 50-acre tract would, under typical residential zoning, support 90 homes on one-half acre lots (with 5 acres for roads and infrastructure), a cluster zoning ordinance might provide for the concentration of the 90 units on one-half of the tract (thus reducing the lot-size requirement) and dedicate the remaining area for open space. Higher development densities are sometimes awarded for clusters to encourage open space preservation. For example, the ordinance might authorize 100 units for the developed one-half of the tract in exchange for the protection of open space in the remainder of the parcel. In order to prevent the future development of the open space area, cluster zoning ordinances often require that most of the undeveloped land be protected by an enforceable conservation easement or deed restriction.

Cluster zoning can be either required or elective as specified in the zoning ordinance. Even if elective, some developers will opt for cluster development, as the resulting open space can often result in higher economic values for the clustered units due to the increased recreational and aesthetic value of their surroundings.

Use for Biodiversity

Cluster zoning is an important tool in any area that is experiencing new development in greenfields (previously undeveloped) areas.[45] *See* Figure 4. For example, in many exurban communities, former farmland and forest land is undergoing conversion to developed uses. Consider cluster zoning's effect on a 40-acre residential development in an area with substantial forest patch size and a small stream corridor. The typical zoning and subdivision ordinance would require the subdivision of land into individual parcels of one-quarter acre with little reference to the natural environment other than prohibiting development directly in the streamway for flooding concerns. Under a cluster zoning approach, the ordinance would require the identification of areas important for forest conservation, habitat, and protection of the riparian corridor and aquatic life (perhaps comprising 15 acres of the tract). These areas might then be designated for conservation while the overall density would be allocated to a set of smaller lots (say one-sixth acre each) grouped apart from the conserved areas. The result would be a development that still has single family detached housing and green space, but whose ecological function has in part been preserved.

Figure 4: Simple Cluster Zoning

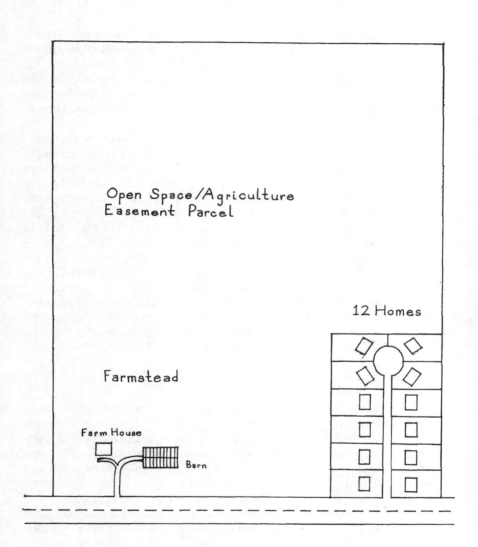

Open Space/Agriculture
Easement Parcel

12 Homes

Farmstead

Farm House

Barn

Road

Drawing by Kathryn Hubler

Cluster requirements that require the protection of the portions of the parcel that are most important for habitat, forest, stream areas, and the like have been called conservation subdivision, a concept that has been popularized by Randall Arendt in a number of books and planning guides.[46] From a biodiversity perspective, cluster zoning is particularly good at maintaining somewhat larger habitat patches than would otherwise be conserved, at preserving linear features such as stream corridors and habitat linkages, and at protecting rare or sensitive areas. It is somewhat less good at allowing natural processes to operate, as the interspersal of housing or other development with natural areas may not be conducive to these processes.

Key Biodiversity Elements

A cluster zoning ordinance for biodiversity should include the following key elements.

1. The ordinance drafter should consider whether, in order to meet the biodiversity objectives, cluster development should be merely authorized or mandated. In areas of substantial conservation concern, in overlay zones protecting landscape features such as wildlife corridors and stream corridors, and in areas with rare and sensitive species, it may be desirable to mandate clustering. If cluster development is to be made optional in these areas under the ordinance, the local government should evaluate the likely impacts if developers choose conventional subdivision and development. If the projected results are unacceptable or cannot be ameliorated by other conservation requirements, then a mandatory approach should be preferred.

2. The cluster development ordinance should explicitly include reference to ecological function as a purpose of the ordinance and a goal to be served in the placement of the clustered development. This is to assist in the ordinance's interpretation and to ensure that the ordinance does not simply result in "hiding homes in the trees" with no ecological benefit.

3. The ordinance should clearly define the characteristics of nonbuildable areas that must be included in the conservation parcel and the characteristics of priority areas to be included in the conservation parcel to the extent possible. Much of the benefit of clustering depends on what is protected—not simply the fact that some land is left undeveloped. It is possible to design cluster developments that have virtually no ecological or biodiversity benefit. The ordinance should identify the features that deserve protection/conservation in order to assure that the goals of the ordinance are achieved.

4. The ordinance should clearly define the authorized uses of the conservation parcel and any maintenance or affirmative obligations associated with it. It should also define by whom the parcel may be held,

and with what easements or other enforcement provisions to assure that the parcel retains its ecological function.

5. Pay attention to the issue of siting cluster developments on the larger landscape. It is especially important to address the relationship of the conservation (open space) parcels to adjacent parcels of land, including nearby parcels that are not part of the development. If conservation areas on adjoining parcels can be aligned, they can better serve the biodiversity conservation objectives of providing habitat corridors and linkages, achieving or maintaining larger patch size, and avoiding land uses that deplete resources over large areas. Unless there is attention to the larger landscape in the ordinance, cluster development can become "pretty sprawl" rather than a tool for conservation. Aligning open space features works best if it has been previously addressed in the comprehensive plan and/or zoning map.

Cluster Development—Calvert County, Maryland

Calvert County, which has the fastest growing population in Maryland, designed and adopted a cluster zoning ordinance to control sprawl and preserve open space and farmland. The ordinance, which went into effect in 1993, implements the county's comprehensive plan and applies to the entire county except town centers. It requires that residential communities outside town centers must be sited and designed to "retain the land's capacity to grow crops, produce timber, provide wildlife habitat, prevent soil erosion, provide recreational open space, contribute to maintaining clean water and air, and preserve rural character."[47]

Clustered development is mandatory for all subdivisions larger than 20 acres. In cases where the parcel is less than 20 acres, clustering is voluntary. The ordinance specifies that lots and roads shall be located in areas where they will have the least effect on forests, sensitive areas, and cropland, and that their location will maintain the rural characteristics of the county. Buildings and roads shall be located in a manner that maximizes the amount of intact contiguous forest area. The ordinance also has a provision for the protection of sensitive areas, prohibiting the building of road and driveway crossings through wetlands, floodplains, steep slopes, and blue line streams.[48]

The maximum number of permitted lots is determined by formula, though lands with substantial sensitive areas may not be able to accommodate the maximum number of lots. Within designated Farm Communities and Resource Preservation Districts, building lots must be grouped onto no more than 20% of the site. Within designated Rural Communities, building lots must be grouped onto no more than 50% of the site. Within Residential R-1 and R-2 Districts, building lots must be placed on no more than 70% of the parcel.

One of the key elements of the cluster zoning ordinance is its protection of open space by covenants or other legal arrangements that assure its preservation in perpetuity. Conservation easements must be deeded to the county or to an approved designee to ensure that designated open space remains undeveloped. Some uses are permitted by deed covenants and owners' certificates. Structures for on-site farming, forestry, and recreation purposes are permitted. Open space land may remain as an undivided parcel or may be subdivided into parcels at least 20 acres in size that still meet the criteria for the open space designation.

Several types of open space are recognized in the ordinance. Farm reserve open space is land that has been cleared for agricultural use in the past and is of adequate size and configuration to continue in that use. Woodland reserve designates forest that is to remain contiguous and undisturbed by development and that is of significant acreage to allow for logging or wildlife management. Conservation open space includes areas with wetlands, floodplains, steep slopes, streams, and their buffers. Community recreation space includes playgrounds and parks. Public access open space is deeded to a government agency or non-profit land trust that agrees to provide public access to the open space for parks, playgrounds, green spaces, or other recreational purposes, and/or for the protection of sensitive areas. Land that is to be developed as a golf course may qualify as public access if it is at least 175 acres with no more than 75% used by the golf course and subject to a number of open space conditions.

Calvert County's mandatory rural clustering is helping to protect segments of the county's rural area. Maryland Department of Planning research has found that the county's cluster development ordinance protects more acres of land than would other development scenarios, but an assessment of biodiversity and habitat values has not been conducted. The design of the ordinance and its recognition of the importance of contiguous forest land and "sensitive areas" in laying out clusters and conservation parcels suggest that positive effects for biodiversity should be expected. Calvert County does have a significant amount of land designated in Maryland's GreenPrint as both core and corridor land.

Incentive Zoning

Description

Incentive zoning is a technique that builds into the zoning ordinance the opportunity for a land developer to obtain additional size or intensity of development in exchange for providing specific features or amenities desired by the community (sometimes called public benefit features). Typically, an incentive zoning ordinance offers a density bonus or a bonus allowing construction of a larger project than would otherwise be authorized, in exchange for the provision of public open spaces, affordable housing, urban design features, transit amenities, or other defined amenities.[49] Some incentive zoning systems authorize cash payments to a fund that is designated to provide the particular amenity (affordable housing funds, pedestrian ways, capital improvements to public spaces serving the immediate area).

Incentive zoning is most commonly used for design features and amenities—arcades, wider sidewalks, entertainment features, public space, affordable housing, and daycare facilities. However, it can be used for conservation purposes as well.

Use for Biodiversity

Incentive zoning might be used, for example, by a township seeking to address the sensitivity of development within an area in the vicinity of a lake. The incentives could be offered for design measures that reduce impervious surfaces, that provide and maintain native vegetation, that avoid fencing of parcels, and that provide a wider than usual lakefront buffer. The incentives could allow smaller lot sizes (greater density) or less extensive infrastructure requirements in return for these additional benefits.

It is important to note that incentive zoning may not be ideal for biodiversity because it renders the provision of the biologically sensitive design features optional. Thus it is more likely to be useful where the baseline biological resources have been protected by other means, including regulatory requirements, and where the desired bonus features are truly additional values. For example, the township could supplement mandatory setback and buffer requirements for parcels adjoining the lake with incentives that reward additional protection for vegetated upland areas that provide greater ecological function and support amphibian reproduction.

The town of Washington, New York, discussed earlier under Zoning Districts, uses incentive zoning to encourage development at less than the maximum density allowed by the zoning ordinance as of right. Landowners who agree to restrict development to one-fifth of the allowable density are authorized to serve the development with private gravel roads rather than paved, town-maintained roads, and may reduce the minimum required road frontage (in order to encourage clustering). The result is larger areas of land in natural uses and more contiguous open space without the downzoning of these areas.[50]

Key Biodiversity Elements

Incentive zoning can be used for biodiversity conservation if it includes the following key elements.

1. The ordinance should establish both the purposes of the incentives and the need for the conservation design features for which incentives will be recognized. The community's need for the conservation measures should be laid out in the comprehensive plan (or subsidiary conservation plans), and then referenced in the incentive zoning ordinance.

2. The ordinance should identify and define the specific conservation design features recognized as the basis for incentives, tailoring them to the specific biodiversity needs in the municipality adopting the ordinance.

3. The ordinance must specify what conservation activities will trigger the award of bonuses. It must specify how the bonuses or incentives will be calculated. It must also specify whether the bonus is awarded by right or is discretionary with the municipality.

4. The ordinance must assure the long-term viability of the conservation design feature that is the basis for the bonus. Specifically, it must contain provisions that will prevent the loss or impairment of the conservation feature. Such provisions may include, if relevant, prohibitions on the privatization of an amenity that needs to be public in order to serve the conservation objective.

Incentive Bonuses—Park City, Utah

The Park City, Utah, Land Management Code includes some incentives in the form of density bonuses for certain open space measures that are above and beyond the base requirements of the city's mandatory steep slope protection and ridge line area protection provisions applicable within the city's Sensitive Area Overlay Zone.

The mandatory requirements for these areas are as follows. Seventy-five percent of the steep slope area (slopes of 15%-40%) must be retained as open space. The remaining 25% may be developed in accordance with the underlying zoning so long as the proposed density will not have a significant adverse visual or environmental effect on the community. The applicant must provide a visual and environmental analysis of the site, based on which the city's Community Development Department may require use of clustered development, dispersed development, or transfer of density to the least sensitive portions of the site. With a sensitive site plan, the applicant may transfer up to 25% of the densities from the open space portion of the site to the developable land, provided that open meadow is retained.[51] On very steep slopes (greater than 40%), 100% shall remain open space; however, up to 10% of the densities otherwise allowed in the zone may be transferred to other portions of the site, subject to a suitability determination.[52] Similarly, the city's provisions protecting ridge line areas allow the planning commission to transfer up to 25% of the densities otherwise allowed on the ridge line area to developable land, so long as it meets a number of suitability criteria.[53]

These base requirements are supplemented by further incentives. Park City's ordinance provides density bonuses for a development form that offers additional environmental and community benefits. On steep slopes, the city's Community Development Department may recommend that the planning commission grant up to a "20% increase" in transferable densities beyond those described above if the applicant:

(1) offers to preserve open space to ensure the long-term protection of a significant environmentally or visually sensitive area in a manner approved by the City; or
(2) provides public access as shown on the Trails Master Plan; or

(3) restores degraded wetlands or environmental areas on the site or makes other significant environmental improvements.[54]

Applicants for development in ridge line areas may also receive up to a 20% increase in transferable densities if they satisfy the criteria referenced above.[55] Park City's ordinance shows how incentives can be used in conjunction with mandatory overlay requirements to encourage the provision of additional, meaningful environmental benefits.

Performance Zoning

Description

Often used for open space and to limit impervious surfaces, performance zoning sets a standard or standards that the development must meet, but allows variation in the type or form of the development itself. While typical zoning ordinances identify specific areas where certain uses are authorized, conditionally authorized, or prohibited, as well as the terms and conditions for such uses in each zone, performance zoning ordinances identify the performance standards that must be met by any development in the zone while allowing variation in the built form.[56]

Performance zoning offers an exchange: the development community receives greater flexibility (and ability to innovate for increased financial return), while the local community assures that its resource concerns are addressed. A performance zoning ordinance may, for example, set standards for natural resource protection, open space, and pervious and impervious surfaces, allowing the developer flexibility in how these standards are met. Some performance zoning ordinances use a point system to track the extent to which a proposed development meets the performance standards. In such a system a certain number of points are needed (either in total or in specific categories) in order to satisfy the ordinance in getting approval for the proposed development action.

Use for Biodiversity

Performance zoning may be particularly useful in protecting rare and sensitive habitats, in allowing a natural disturbance regime to continue, and in minimizing the introduction and spread of invasive exotic species and the introduction of pollutants. It may also be useful in providing for mitigation of habitat loss.

Performance zoning can enhance the effectiveness of other conservation measures. For example, consider a community that has acquired a lakeshore or prairie area as a publicly protected area. The community recognizes that simply holding the most sensitive land in conservation status will not fully protect its function and utility for the community. On the other hand, the community is not ready to severely limit development on the surrounding private lands. Performance zoning provides an approach that can serve the community's goals. The community may zone the privately owned area adjacent to the publicly owned land as a buffer or conservation overlay zone. But instead of prescribing precisely what uses and densities are authorized as of right, the ordinance sets up a system of points under which uses will be evaluated. Points are awarded for: preservation of the town's vista over the lakeshore or prairie; minimization of impervious surface; passage for wildlife; vegetation compatible with the protected area; and avoidance of the introduction of chemicals. The resulting developments might take a number of potential forms (even allowing mixed commercial and residential uses), but the functional protection of the sensitive area will be assured by the performance standards.

Of course, ordinances establishing standard zoning districts may also be written to include performance standards that are significant for biodiversity conservation. There is not a bright line distinction between performance standards and performance zoning. The latter tends to be more flexible as to uses and design specifications.

Key Biodiversity Elements

Performance zoning can be used for biodiversity conservation with the following key elements.

1. In drafting the ordinance, be sure to include enough area within the performance zoning district to accomplish the ecological objectives that the plan has established.

2. Realize that you can't predict the timing of development, so don't use this tool for issues that are time-critical.

3. Clearly define the conservation elements for which credit is given. This will require careful work with conservation biologists or others to assure that the measures are well-tailored to the objectives.

4. Use this tool only if you expect to have and maintain a professional planning staff that is sophisticated enough to evaluate what is being proposed as development occurs.

Performance Zoning—Milford Township, Pennsylvania

Milford Township, in Bucks County, Pennsylvania, has worked to control growth and protect natural resources through its performance zoning and development districts. The township has worked with the Natural Lands Trust and the Bucks County Planning Commission to incorporate conservation planning into its land use regulations. Specifically, the township's performance standards zoning works with its subdivision and land development provisions to protect contiguous open space and natural resources.[57]

Milford Township's natural resource and open space protection objectives are implemented through performance standards defined by zoning ordinance.[58] The environmental performance standards contain critical natural resources protection standards that prohibit or limit the impact of development in areas encompassing the particular resource. Flood plains and flood plain soils must be 100% protected and no development, other than minor road crossings, may occur in these areas. Wetlands, lakes, ponds, and watercourses must also be 100% protected. Lake shores (within 300 feet from the shoreline) must be 90% protected. Wetland margins and pond shores within 100 feet from the shoreline must be 80% protected. On wooded sites, not more than 20% of woodlands on a site may be "altered, regraded, cleared or built upon." In steep slope areas, depending on the degree of the slope, not more than 15 to 40% of the areas may be altered, regraded, cleared, or built upon. There is also a tree protection zone. The area within the drip line of the tree canopy shall not be disturbed during construction.[59] The performance standards provisions also include guidelines on site capacity calculations, which include open space ratios to support natural resources. The calculation guidelines include minimum and standard open space and active recreation land considerations. Open space standards apply to all major residential subdivisions and all nonresidential subdivisions and land developments.[60]

The township's recently revised subdivision and land development ordinance lays out the procedures for the development and subdivision process to assure that the performance standards of the zoning ordinance are met. The procedures include a preapplication meeting, sketch plan submission and review, and an extensive review process during which township planners review site plans.[61] The process for assessing compliance with open space performance standards includes a resource inventory and a four-step design process. The first of the four steps is the delineation of open space and development areas, including "conservation areas" in the required open space. Infrastructure and lot lines must be laid out to avoid fragmentation or adverse impacts on the open space. The ordinance requires that the open space area must be contiguous and interconnected, that it not include parcels smaller than three acres, have a length-to-width ratio of less than 4:1,[62] nor be less than 75 feet in width, with exceptions. The open space must be interconnected whenever possible to provide a "continuous network of open space within and adjoining the development."[63] These provisions are addressed to the issue of "edge,"assuring that habitat parcels have some integrity while also distinguishing between corridors and core areas. The ordinance includes open space planting requirements, including forestation standards for open space (680 trees per acre, planted in a random pattern).[64]

Milford Township's zoning and planning performance requirements generally result in clustered development projects. For example, a recent developer refrained from creating a cookie-cutter development and instead built a small clustered development. In the process, the developer protected the required open space, including woods surrounding Hazelbach Creek, part of a larger watershed, through conservation easements and use restrictions.[65] Key to the township's work to protect open space resources are the site calculations and resource protection standards in the zoning ordinance. In addition, the design provisions in the subdivision regulation play a major role in the placement and function of open space, helping to ensure contiguous natural areas suitable for biodiversity. In developing its ordinances, the township has relied on mapping of the jurisdiction and adjacent jurisdictions that identify critical areas and secondary conservation areas for protection.

Traditional Neighborhood Development

Description

Traditional Neighborhood Development (TND) is an alternative zoning practice that encourages mixed use developments in compact areas, mimicking the designs that prevailed in towns throughout America before World War II. TND zoning provisions generally contain much more specific design standards than conventional zoning. TND districts typically emphasize mixing commercial and residential uses and specify design elements such as grid street patterns, ample sidewalks, maximum setback limitations, narrow streets, and community open spaces. Unlike conventional zoning, which separates residential and commercial land uses, thus encouraging sprawl and use of the automobile, TND neighborhoods are designed to be compact, efficient, and pedestrian-friendly.

Use for Biodiversity

TND development can be useful for biodiversity by allowing the denser development of a parcel and/or redevelopment of a previously developed area, thus slowing the impetus for sprawl into greenfields areas. The ordinance may also ensure that design elements that support biodiversity are included. For example, a local government could adopt a TND ordinance allowing such development as a conditional use in some zones. The required design features could include the preservation of grass swales and drainage ways that use vegetation rather than concrete; they could also provide for a "commons" area with ecological features. By limiting sprawl and confining development to smaller, denser areas, TNDs can preserve habitat by avoiding fragmentation.

Note that these communities, if constructed in greenfields areas, need to be sited appropriately because they too can contribute to biodiversity impairment just as traditional sprawl developments can.

Key Biodiversity Elements

Traditional neighborhood development ordinances can be drafted to support biodiversity if they contain the following key elements.

1. The ordinance should provide for relatively dense development, but should also include some minimization of impervious surface so that water flow and quality is not unnecessarily impaired. The design provisions can include such requirements as rain gardens, wetland areas, and vegetation requirements.

2. The ordinance should assure that parkland within the development is not entirely developed and that there is some attempt to maintain ecological function. Inclusion of areas for passive recreation, wildlife,

ponds and wetlands, and the like can be an important part of a success-fully drafted ordinance.

3. The ordinance should give some attention to the linkages of developments with surrounding lands. The placement of TNDs on the landscape is important, and where it is possible to maintain intact habitat patches and corridors and connections, the ordinance should require that such factors be included in the development design.

Traditional Neighborhood Development—Civano, Arizona

Civano, a new town within the city of Tucson, Arizona, was designed to blend traditional neighborhood design with advanced technology to reduce energy and water consumption, reduce vehicle traffic and solid waste generation, and integrate working and living environments. Featuring energy efficiency and solar energy, the development of 2,800 homes and offices and industrial facilities is expected to cover 818 acres.[66]

One-third of the land is open space. The open space includes natural areas as well as more developed community orchards, linear parks, pedestrian trails, bike paths, and other recreational facilities.[67] Civano uses native Sonoran desert plants for landscaping of open space and common areas, and the local nursery offers homeowner workshops in xeriscaping and desert gardening. The nursery salvaged and replanted approximately 65% of the major desert vegetation during the development of the town. The xeriscaping program reused "thousands of foothills paloverdes, velvet mesquites, creosotes, saguaro and fishhook (barrel) cacti, and a host of smaller plants important to the area's ecology. These salvaged plants have been replanted onsite and on individual lots."[68]

The town's guiding development principles—the Integrated Method of Performance and Cost Tracking (IMPACT) for Sustainable Development Standards—are intended to balance growth, housing affordability, and the natural environment.[69] The town's designers mixed commercial and residential areas, included elements of traditional design such as front porches, and followed environmentally oriented construction and operating principles. In support of the planned community, the city of Tucson rewrote codes and invested in the underlying infrastructure, becoming a partner in the development. While clearly a conversion of land from natural desert to human habitation and mixed uses, the Civano approach takes into account some elements of biodiversity on the site-specific (rather than regional) scale, indicating that urbanization using traditional neighborhood design can accommodate to at least some degree native plants and landscape conservation.

Conclusion

While planning and zoning set the goals and ground rules for land development, many of the important decisions are made at the stage of subdivision and development approval. Ideally, subdivision and land development ordinances are dovetailed with zoning ordinances (as in the case of Milford Township, above). The next chapter examines ways in which land development approval processes can be designed to support biodiversity.

Chapter Four Endnotes

1. For tables identifying which types of local jurisdictions are authorized or required to prepare comprehensive plans by state laws, see ENVIRONMENTAL LAW INSTITUTE (ELI) & DEFENDERS OF WILDLIFE, PLANNING FOR BIODIVERSITY: AUTHORITIES IN STATE LAND USE LAWS 10, 19 (2003), *available at* http://www.elistore.org/reports_detail.asp?ID=10917 (last visited Dec. 1, 2003).

2. GROWING SMART LEGISLATIVE GUIDEBOOK §§7-201 to 7-216 (Stuart Meck ed., American Planning Ass'n 2002). Unfortunately, the guidebook makes natural resources an optional, rather than required plan element, an approach that does not reflect current best practice. The model language does, however, require comprehensive planning for "critical and sensitive areas" in most instances.

3. ELI & DEFENDERS OF WILDLIFE, *supra* note 1.

4. The town of Warwick, New York, prepared a comprehensive plan that took into account the development potential of the incorporated village of Warwick (over which it had no jurisdiction), and entered into an intermunicipal agreement with the village on annexation and zoning. John R. Nolon, Golden *and Its Emanations: The Surprising Origins of Smart Growth*, 35 URB. LAW. 15, 36-42 (2003).

5. Contact state chapters of The Nature Conservancy. *See* The Nature Conservancy, *North America: The United States*, *at* http://nature.org/wherewework/northamerica/states/ (last visited Dec. 4, 2003). Ecoregional planning is the subject of a new book that also contains good information on conservation planning at multiple scales. CRAIG R. GROVES, DRAFTING A CONSERVATION BLUEPRINT (Island Press 2003).

6. Some of the relevant concepts and some threshold values are identified in ELI, CONSERVATION THRESHOLDS FOR LAND USE PLANNERS (2003) (explaining and giving some ranges of considerations for habitat patches including size and configuration, quantity of habitat in a landscape, edge effects, riparian buffers, and habitat connectivity, based on a survey of scientific papers).

7. The plan was revised in accordance with state law requirements for regular plan review and updates. N.J. STAT. ANN. §§40:55D-1 et seq. (West).

8. 2002 Master Plan, Goals and Objectives, Land Use Plan Element, Conservation Plan Element, Township of Hopewell, Mercer County, New Jersey. Adopted as revised on May 23, 2002, memorialized on June 13, 2002 [hereinafter 2002 Master Plan].

9. *Id.* at Goals and Objectives, Land Use Plan Element, Conservation Plan Element.

10. *Id.* at Conservation Plan Element, Summary.

11. For more information on forest conservation by local governments, see the discussion on Forest Conservation/Tree Protection, *infra* Chapter Seven.

12. 2002 Master Plan, *supra* note 8, at Conservation Plan Element, Forest Resources and Native Vegetation.

13. Telephone Interview with Dr. Ted Stiles, Township Environmental Commission (Jan. 14, 2003).

14. 2002 Master Plan, *supra* note 8, at Conservation Plan Element, Threatened and Endangered Plant and Animal Species.

15. *Id.*

16. Telephone Interview with Scott Clark, Albemarle County Planning Staff (Sept. 25, 2002).

17. Albemarle County Comprehensive Plan, Chapter Two, Natural Resources and Cultural Assets (adopted Mar. 3, 1999), at 73-86, *available at* http://www.albemarle.org/department.asp?department=planning&relpage=3003 (last visited Dec. 19, 2003).

18. *Id.*

19. *Id.* at 84.

20. *Id.* at 85.

21. *See supra* note 13 and Telephone Interview with Scott Clark, Albemarle County Planning Staff (Oct. 3, 2002).

22. *See* CHRISTOPHER DUERKSEN ET AL., HABITAT PROTECTION PLANNING: WHERE THE WILD THINGS ARE 32 (Planning Advisory Service Report No. 470/471) (American Planning Ass'n 1997).

23. Reed v. Rootstown Township Bd. of Zoning Appeals, 458 N.E.2d 940 (Ohio 1984).

24. Town of Beverly Shores v. Bagnall, 590 N.E.2d 1059 (Ind. 1992).

25. Cluster Zoning is discussed *infra* notes 45-48.

26. Joel S. Russell, *A New Generation of Rural Land Use Laws*, ZONING NEWS, July 1996, at 1-2.

27. City of Boise, *Planning and Development Services*, *at* http://www.cityofboise.org/pds/comp.shtml (last visited Dec. 4, 2003).

28. BOISE, IDAHO, FOOTHILLS PLANNED DEVELOPMENT ORDINANCE, CITY CODE §11-06-05.7.5.C (2000), *available at* http://www.cityofboise.org/pds/Comp-Plan/Foothills/Foothills_Planned_Dev_ord.pdf (last visited Dec. 4, 2003).

29. *Id.* §11-06-05.7.3.

30. BOISE, IDAHO, MUNICIPAL CODE, ZONING CLASSIFICATIONS, §11-04-09 (2002), *available at* http://www.cityofboise.org/city_clerk/codes/1104.pdf (last visited Dec. 4, 2003).

31. FALMOUTH, MASS., WILDLIFE CORRIDOR PROTECTION BYLAW §4600 (1988).

32. *Id.*

33. Telephone Interview with Brian Currie, Town of Falmouth (Aug. 20, 2002).

34. *See* CENTER FOR RURAL PENNSYLVANIA, ZONING FOR FARMING (1995).

35. Living Places, *Agriculture in Berks County: 1775-1900, at* http://www.livingplaces.net/pa/berks/historicdistricts/berksfarms/farmsinberkscounty.html (last visited Dec. 4, 2003); *see* CLYDE MYERS & CHERYL AUCHENBACH, EFFECTIVE AGRICULTURAL ZONING—ONE TOOL TO HELP SAVE AN INDUSTRY (2001).

36. PA. MUNICIPALITIES PLANNING CODE, Act 247, §604(3). *See also* 53 PA. CONST. STAT. ANN. §10604(3).

37. In 2001, over 191,000 acres were under permanent agricultural conservation easements statewide, approaching 250,000 acres by the end of 2002. PENNSYLVANIA DEPARTMENT OF AGRICULTURE, FARMLAND PRESERVATION, PENNSYLVANIA IS THE LEADER, ANNUAL REPORT TO THE GENERAL ASSEMBLY, 2000-2001 (2002), *available at* http://www.agriculture.state.pa.us/agriculture/lib/agriculture/2001_annual_report.pdf (last visited Dec. 4, 2003).

38. BERKS COUNTY LAND PRESERVATION STATISTICS (1997).

39. MYERS & AUCHENBACH, *supra* note 35.

40. BETHEL TOWNSHIP, PA., ZONING ORDINANCE OF 2000 §610.04-.06.

41. *Id.* §640.04-.05.

42. *Id.*

43. *Id.* §640.07-.08.

44. *Id.* §620.05.

45. The U.S. Environmental Protection Agency (EPA) has published resources for a model cluster development ordinance intended to protect open space. *See* U.S. EPA, *Open Space Development, at* http://www.epa.gov/owow/nps/ordinance/openspace. htm (last visited Dec. 4, 2003).

46. RANDALL ARENDT ET AL., RURAL BY DESIGN (American Planning Ass'n 1994); RANDALL ARENDT, GROWING GREENER: PUTTING CONSERVATION INTO LOCAL PLANS AND ORDINANCES (Island Press 1999).

47. CALVERT COUNTY, MD., ZONING REGULATIONS ch. 5.

48. Telephone Interview with Olivia Vidotto-Hiner, Calvert County Department of Planning and Zoning (Aug. 6, 2002).

49. *See generally* MARYA MORRIS, INCENTIVE ZONING: MEETING URBAN DESIGN AND AFFORDABLE HOUSING OBJECTIVES (Planning Advisory Service Report No. 494) (American Planning Ass'n 2000).

50. Russell, *supra* note 26.

51. PARK CITY, UTAH, MUNICIPAL CORP. MUNICIPAL CODE §15-2.21-4(H).

52. *Id.* §15-2.21-4(I).

53. *Id.* §15-2.21-5(C).

54. *Id.* §15-2.21-4(K).

55. *Id.* §15-2.21-5(D).

56. LANE KENDIG, PERFORMANCE ZONING (1980).

57. Milford Township, *Planning Direction, at* http://www.milfordtownship.org (last visited Dec. 4, 2003).

58. QUAKERTOWN AREA ZONING ORDINANCE OF 1975 (as amended by Ord. 099 (July 18, 1995) in accordance with a 1992 comprehensive plan). The comprehensive plan was adopted as a multimunicipal comprehensive plan and includes Milford Township and five other municipalities. *See* Milford Township, *Open Space Plan, at* http:// www.milfordtownship.org/pdfs/os-plan.pdf (last visited Dec. 4, 2003).

59. QUAKERTOWN AREA ZONING ORDINANCE OF 1975, art. V, §504.

60. *Id.* §501.

61. MILFORD TOWNSHIP, PA., SUBDIVISION AND LAND DEVELOPMENT ORDINANCE, art. IV (2002), *available at* http://www.milfordtownship.org/pdfs/ord-123-saldo.pdf (last visited Dec. 4, 2003).

62. Although the ordinance language is arguably ambiguous, the ordinance apparently seeks to avoid long, narrow, open space areas other than corridors, which would actually mean avoiding ratios greater than 4:1, e.g., 5:1, 6:1.

63. *See supra* note 61, art. V, §522.

64. *Id.* §520(d)(3).

65. Telephone Interview with Jeff Vey, Milford Township (Nov. 27, 2002).

66. Congress for the New Urbanism, *at* http://www.cnu.org (last visited Dec. 4, 2003). *See also* Mark Smith, *Civano: A Report From the Field*, ENVTL. DESIGN & CONSTRUC-

TION, Jan. 2001, *available at* http://www.edcmag.com/edc/cda/articleinformation/ features/bnp__features__item/0,,19210,00+en-uss_01dbc.html (last visited Dec. 22, 2003).

67. Florida Sustainable Communities Center, *Civano: New Thinking for a New Town, at* http://sustainable.state.fl.us/fdi/fscc/news/world/9904/civ.htm (last visited Dec. 4, 2003).

68. 3 PATHWAYS 1 (1999) *available at* http://www.pathnet.org/sf.asp?id=450 (last visited Dec. 22, 2003).

69. Civano, *at* http://www.civano.com (last visited Dec. 4, 2003).

Chapter Five—Development Approvals

Some kinds of land use regulations are tied to an application review and approval process. These include subdivisions, applications for rezoning, and site plan approvals. Application requirements and standards can provide opportunities to address biodiversity conservation at the site level. This chapter covers:

- Development Applications and Information Requirements;
- Planned Unit Development (PUD);
- Exactions and Proffers; and
- Subdivision Regulation.

Development Applications and Information Requirements

Description

Many jurisdictions require the submission of surveys and environmental information in connection with any application for development. A number of jurisdictions have prescribed the submission of specific biodiversity and habitat information.

Use for Biodiversity

The incorporation of information requirements into an application process is very useful in areas where specific habitat areas, species, and biodiversity concerns have been previously identified in the comprehensive plan and zoning ordinance. This information-gathering tool particularly serves the need to protect rare habitat elements and species. It also provides information to support compensation for unavoidable habitat losses or impairments.

Information requirements can be adopted by ordinance even where a comprehensive plan does not specifically identify biodiversity concerns, where the existence of some basis for development concern has recently become known. However, the ordinance will need to link the requirement to an appropriate part of the zoning or subdivision ordinance.

Key Biodiversity Elements

Information requirements should address the following elements:

1. The ordinance drafter and local governing body should consider whether to make the information requirement jurisdictionwide, or whether to link it to particular districts identified on the zoning map. It is probable that some basic biodiversity information is important for all locations, but that other (more specific) information is needed in

particular overlay areas or sensitive landscape regions.

2. The ordinance should be written so that it specifically requires the applicant to consult state natural heritage data, state green infrastructure maps, and other available information. The ordinance should ensure that these information sources are consulted by the applicant, but not be drafted so narrowly that other relevant information can be ignored by the applicant without violating the ordinance.

3. The ordinance should be written to ensure that the applicant identifies habitat types, connectivity and linkages, waterways, and other features on the landscape that may affect the development's likely effect on biodiversity. The ordinance should require baseline inventories of identified natural features.

Wildlife Impact Report—Boulder County, Colorado

In 1999, Boulder County amended its Land Use Code to add a requirement to ensure that developers consider and provide information on habitat to be affected by proposed land development activities. The wildlife provisions require that "all land use development actions which require a development impact report . . . shall be required to include a wildlife impact report whenever the property is located within" certain designated areas. The relevant development actions include subdivisions, PUDs, special review and limited impact special review approvals, rezonings, and exemption applications. The designated areas within which the wildlife impact report is required for these applications include, among others:

- a critical wildlife habitat, a significant natural community, a rare plant area, or a natural corridor as designated on environmental resources maps of the county's comprehensive plan;
- a natural area or natural landmark, or a Boulder Valley Natural Ecosystem as designated by plan;
- a critical habitat for state or federally designated threatened or endangered species; or
- an area that has been determined to serve as significant habitat for species of special county concern.[1]

The report must be prepared by a wildlife expert approved by and retained by the County Parks and Open Space Department. The report must inventory species, assess the property's habitat status, review possible mitigation measures, and must recommend whether the proposal can proceed without causing material adverse impact on species of special county concern or its significant habitat and if so, on what basis the development proposal can avoid such impact.

The ordinance ensures that the county has sufficient detailed information to address and anticipate concerns and also ensures that the developer has the information necessary to take into account appropriate issues of design in undertaking to submit a development application.

CHAPTER FIVE—DEVELOPMENT APPROVALS

PUD

Description

PUD provisions permit large tracts to be developed, or groups of tracts to be assembled and developed, in a more flexible manner than would have been permitted by the underlying zoning. Because the development is planned and reviewed as an entity, the developer may be able to achieve better site planning by altering the use, density, and design requirements in the zoning law. There is no standard definition of a PUD, as local governments' use of the technique has resulted in a range of options for more flexible development. These include relaxation of minimum lot size requirements, permitting mixed residential and commercial land use, or allowing greater design flexibility. In exchange, developers are often required to compensate for the impacts of their projects by leaving more open space, meeting the infrastructure needs of the development, or offering other community facilities and services.

PUD regulations are either found in the zoning ordinance or, if no density or use changes are authorized, the subdivision control ordinance. PUD regulations contain standards and approval criteria while maintaining a level of flexibility to permit the developer and municipality to negotiate the rules and conditions for development. This technique is applicable primarily to large developments, as small-scale developers cannot afford the front-end legal and design costs of a PUD and generally opt to follow the path of least resistance under prevailing zoning rules.

Use for Biodiversity

PUDs can be extremely important for biodiversity conservation because they enable a developer and local government to address the consequences of a large, sometimes multiphase development holistically. Applying PUD standards also can help overcome the evils of parcelization that often result from by-right subdivision of land without regard to specific landscape features. The consideration of a large tract at one time makes it possible to identify and provide for conservation of habitat patches, to define and conserve connections between areas important for conservation, to limit the introduction and spread of exotic species, and to fulfill a number of the other considerations discussed in Chapter Two.

Because PUDs must be defined by ordinance, the local government may define conservation objectives that a PUD must meet. Indeed, the ordinance may even define a category of "conservation PUD" as an option. The critical decision to make in drafting the ordinance, however, is to assure that the PUD requirements are not structured in such a way that no one would ever reasonably apply for a PUD. The advantages of PUD applications as well as the conditions and limitations need to be apparent.

Key Biodiversity Elements

PUD provisions should include the following key elements to ensure conservation:

1. The PUD provisions should explicitly define biodiversity objectives and provide some clear standards based on the conservation guidelines. Many of the approaches discussed above under overlay zoning, cluster zoning, and performance zoning are relevant to PUD development.

2. The ordinance should expressly address landscape connections and adjacent land uses. The issue of how the PUD relates to the surrounding landscape is important in the biodiversity context, just as in the transportation context. Thus, the ordinance should require assessment of these spatial relationships and should require connection of conserved areas within the PUD and with adjacent habitat patches and corridors.

3. The PUD ordinance should define mitigation standards for biodiversity resources that will be unavoidably impaired by the development.

4. The PUD ordinance cannot make up for bad underlying zoning. If a PUD is hard to do and has numerous conservation requirements while by-right development does not, it is quite possible that no one will undertake the PUD option. Both the underlying zoning and the PUD provisions should be clear about desired conservation goals and conditions, as well as development goals.

PUD—City of Bellevue, Washington

The city of Bellevue, Washington, encourages the conservation of open space through its PUD regulation. The PUD is a development option under which the city may permit a "variety in type, design, and arrangement of structures." It allows for innovations and special features that include "the location of structures, conservation of natural land features, conservation of energy and efficient utilization of open space."[2] The city may approve a PUD plan if it is consistent with the city's comprehensive plan and if the PUD will produce a development that is better than that which would result from standard development under the zoning ordinance. The city considers a number of factors under the regulation when approving a PUD. These include: placement, type, or reduced bulk of structures; conservation of interconnected usable open space; recreation facilities; other public facilities; conservation of natural features; aesthetic features and harmonious design; or energy-efficient site design or building features.[3]

The "open space and recreation space" provision requires that at least 40% of the gross land area must be retained or developed as open space as defined in the city's land use code.[4] But the ordinance is drafted to ensure that both recreational and biological goals are addressed. At least 10% of the gross land area must be common recreation space, and at least 20% of the gross land area must be nonrecreation open space. The city may require a performance or maintenance assurance device to assure the retention and continued maintenance of all open and recreation space.[5]

The city's definition of open space encompasses "land area unoccupied by buildings, traffic circulation roads, or parking areas, including, but not limited to woodlands, fields, sidewalks, walkways, landscape areas, gardens, courtyards, or lawns."[6] Because of the breadth of the definition, the PUD provision by itself does not invariably protect biodiversity. However, developers of a PUD complying with Washington State's critical areas law[7] will usually protect the state-mandated critical areas as part of the identified open space required in the PUD program. Together, the two tools can result in the protection of biologically important space that is consolidated and undeveloped—including undeveloped parkland that supports habitat.[8]

In PUDs critical areas are usually protected in tracts that are owned in common among all property owners and remain relatively consolidated, unfenced, and undisturbed. In contrast, in non-PUD small to medium subdivisions, state-required critical areas are often preserved as native growth protection easements on individual lots. These individual lots are often fenced or otherwise disturbed, reducing the viability of the native habitat.[9]

Bellevue staff note that the PUD program could be strengthened somewhat by modifying the open space definition to emphasize natural features and interconnected areas.

Exactions and Proffers

Description

Exactions, impact fees, and proffers are means by which local governments assure that land developers provide for public services and infrastructure needed to support the development's incremental demands for such services and infrastructure. Because land development can produce additional costs for the host locality—including need for roads, water, public services, schools, parkland, and open space—many municipalities grant subdivision approval (or site plan approval) or rezoning in connection with a development proposal only where the landowner satisfies requirements for these services.

In states that allow "exactions" the local government by ordinance imposes conditions upon approvals that may require the dedication of land, construction of certain infrastructure improvements, adoption of compensatory environmental mitigation measures, and/or sometimes payment of money (in-lieu of dedication) to support these investments where they occur off-site.

Where compelled payment of money is provided for in the ordinance, this is known as an "impact fee" rather than an exaction. The amount and usage of the fee must be linked to the provision of some identified service, acquisition of some identified land, or funding for a capital improvement related to the development's effect. Impact fees often apply to transportation improvements, park lands and facilities, and school funding, but may apply to other purposes as authorized by state law and the local ordinance.[10]

In states using the "proffer" system, the local government may not impose dedications or exactions but instead negotiates with the developer over what the developer may be willing to contribute to the community and how the developer may be willing to modify or mitigate the impacts of the development. In practice, proffers can resemble exactions because developers desiring expeditious approval of their site plans or rezoning requests agree to address anticipated adverse impacts in order to satisfy the local governmental body. Proffers are not allowed in some states, e.g., Tennessee, where they are characterized as "contract zoning," which improperly constrains the local legislative function. Other states specifically allow proffers or even more detailed bargains between developers and local governments, known as development agreements.[11]

Exactions, impact fees, and proffers are governed by state enabling acts (or home-rule charters), by local ordinances establishing such provisions, and by constitutional requirements. The constitutional requirements covering exactions of land include requirements that the exaction have a "rational nexus" to the development activity and that it be "roughly proportional" to the impact of the development.[12]

Use for Biodiversity

Exactions, impact fees, proffers, and development agreements may be quite important in assuring the functional protection of areas important for biodiversity. Requirements might include dedication of wildlife corridors and open space, limitations or offsets for impervious surfaces and stormwater management, requirements for vegetation conservation areas, establishing native plants, xeriscaping, and wildlife plantings. Provisions may also require mitigation for loss in forest cover and tree canopy, and agreements to minimize tree disturbance or contribute to a reforestation fund. These land use tools may be used to address any of the conservation guidelines identified in Chapter Two. However, it is extremely important that they be closely linked to foreseeable impacts of the development on the resources of the larger community.

Key Biodiversity Elements

Exactions, impact fees and proffers can serve biodiversity objectives if several key elements are addressed:

1. It is very important to articulate a rational nexus to the development impact. Where the ordinance provides for dedications of land it is especially important to document the basis for determining the proportionality of the dedication, backed by some articulated methodology. Where the ordinance provides for an impact fee, the ordinance must document the basis for determining the fee, exactly how the funds are to be maintained and expended, and what connection the fee has to the

impacts of the development. All of these goals can best be met by solid biological studies in advance of development and the preparation of a sound resource inventory at the comprehensive plan and zoning ordinance adoption stage.

2. The goals to be served by the exaction, impact fee, or proffer should be identified in the jurisdiction's comprehensive plan. The plan serves as the basis for the ordinance.

3. For impact fees, the conservation expenditures should be included in the capital improvement budget of the local government. The fees should be designated to particular purposes (such as reforestation, corridor assembly and protection, wildlife crossings and related capital expenditures, or invasive species eradication, for example).

Proffers—Loudoun County, Virginia

Proffers are among the tools being used in Virginia's fastest growing county to address some of the issues surrounding biodiversity and conservation.[13] From 1990 to 2000, Loudoun County's population increased 97%, putting strain on the county's many high quality plant and animal habitats.[14] According to the Virginia Department of Conservation's Natural Heritage Biological and Conservation Data system, the county's natural resources include rare, threatened, and endangered plants and animal species as well as numerous exemplary natural communities, habitats, and ecosystems.[15] Until recent amendments to the zoning ordinance reduced prospective densities and required clustering in Loudoun County's rural area, proffers were used as a primary tool for addressing major development impacts to habitat and conservation lands.

Loudoun County's comprehensive plan forms the basis for evaluating land use proposals and for amending zoning and subdivision ordinances. The plan describes the county's ecological priorities in a chapter called the Green Infrastructure, which defines three goals.[16] The first goal is conservation, which means creating a stronger relationship between natural and built environments. The second goal is preservation, which means retaining and protecting existing environmental, natural, and heritage resources. The third goal is restoration, which means adding to the Green Infrastructure wherever possible.

The Green Infrastructure chapter targets four groups of distinct and valuable "green" components. The first category is Natural Resource Assets. It includes river and stream corridors; scenic rivers and the Potomac River; surface and groundwater resources; geologic and soil resources; forests, trees, and vegetation; and plant and wildlife habitats.[17] The goal for this group of elements is preservation and, wherever practical, restoration of their natural state. The second group is Heritage Resource Assets, consisting of historic and archeological resources, and scenic areas and corridors.[18] The third group is Open Space Assets. It includes greenways and trails, parks and recreation, public school sites, and open space easements; this group of elements can enhance the vibrancy of communities by providing public interaction with nature and opportunities for outdoor activity.[19] The fourth group is Complementary Elements and includes air quality, lighting and the night sky, and the aural environment.[20] For each of these resources, the county has established policies and practices to promote conservation, preservation, and protection.

Loudoun County has used proffers to influence development and offset some of its impacts. Proffers are voluntary commitments that a developer makes to the county, which offset impacts and assist in improving the public infrastructure.[21] This tool has been a part of Loudoun County's means to implement its vision for ecological recovery. When a developer wants to develop in a way that differs in density or use from the current zoning ordinance, she or he must make a legislative application for rezoning. At this point, the county can request a proffer, that is, ask the developer to integrate certain features, or provide certain amenities in exchange for permission for the subdivision. In Virginia, a county may not require a developer to provide these additional features or amenities in exchange for rezoning, but may negotiate with the developer by offering favorable treatment in the application process.

There are three main categories of proffers that the county may seek from a developer, depending on the proposed development and the needs of the area in question.[22] The first type of proffer is open space.[23] This is an agreement by the developer to set aside and maintain natural area in its natural state. These areas can be a particular ecological feature, such as mountainside, forest, and/or steep slopes. The second type of proffer is conservation design.[24] This refers to design features that are written into the development plan to integrate natural or ecologically preferable features such as greenways, native plants, or pervious land cover.[25] The third category of proffer is capital facilities.[26] These are contributions by the developer, in money or in kind, to contribute to the infrastructure demands created by the new development, such as schools, roads, or parks.

The process for negotiating proffers is relatively straightforward. The county publishes its preferences for proffers in the Comprehensive Plan so developers know ahead of time what kinds of proffers are likely to be accepted or at least desired by the Planning Commission. The developer submits a Concept Development Plan, which is essentially his or her first offer. The Planning Commission staff will review the plan to ensure compliance with any regulations and to determine how the plan will affect the values expressed in the Green Infrastructure chapter. If more information or data is required in order to reach an informed decision about the site, the county may request that the developer conduct additional studies such as a forest assessment, a floodplain study, or an archeological study to determine whether the development will adversely affect a sensitive feature. Because the commission is also interested in mitigating the costs of capital facilities, such as roads, it may require the developer to conduct a transportation analysis to determine whether the site can handle the additional traffic or to what extent additional transportation infrastructure will be needed. These studies also contribute to the commission's overall knowledge about the ecology of the county. Once all of the data are in, the developer and commission staff negotiate over additional proffers. Though the commission is responsible for stewardship over the land and, thus, has some leeway in negotiations, it is required to approve a plan if it reasonably complies with the comprehensive plan policies and the zoning ordinance. Once the county approves the rezoning request, the proffer agreement becomes an enforceable zoning regulation and runs with the land until a subsequent rezoning.[27]

The increase in development pressure over the last decade has led to recognition that most residents of the county now favor greater protection of the county's ecological integrity and quality of life.[28] Because the use of proffers to promote the Green Infrastructure is fairly recent, it is difficult to evaluate the impact of this tool on biodiversity. Moreover, proffers are essentially a passive tool that come into play only where rezoning is sought. Other land use tools, including overlay districts, clustering, river buffers, steep slope protection, incentives, purchase of development rights, and public acquisition of lands, are essential components of an overall strategy to conserve, preserve, and restore Loudoun County's biological and historical heritage. In recent years, the County Board of Supervisors has directed the Planning Commission to give special emphasis to the protection of Natural Resource Assets. In 2003 this led to the adoption of substantial new zoning ordinances that more strictly protect rural areas of the county. But in late 2003 opponents of the new ordinances ousted several of the board members. Proffers will likely continue to play a role in conservation, whatever the fate of the conservation-oriented zoning ordinances.

Exactions and Impact Fees—Placer County, California

Fast-growing Placer County in California's gold country defined a policy for parks and recreational facilities in its 1994 General Plan, establishing a policy to achieve and maintain a standard of 5 acres of improved parkland and 5 acres of "passive recreation area or open space" for every 1,000 residents.[29] The plan also established goals related to water quality and biodiversity.[30] The open space portion of the plan is implemented in part by Placer County's adoption of an ordinance under California's Quimby Act, which allows cities or counties to require the dedication of land or impose a requirement of payment of in-lieu fees, or a combination of both, for park or recreational purposes as a condition to the approval of a parcel map. The Quimby Act provides that the amount of land dedicated or fees paid shall be based upon residential density but not exceeding 3 acres of park area per 1,000 persons within the subdivision (or 5 acres if the existing amount of parkland exceeds that ratio). The land and impact fees exacted through the program ordinance are only to be used to develop new or rehabilitate existing park or recreational facilities to serve the subdivision.[31]

Under its comprehensive plan, Placer County seeks to exceed the Quimby Act goals by achieving and maintaining 5 acres of improved parkland *and* 5 acres of passive recreation area or open space per 1,000 new residents. This can be important for biodiversity as the county considers protected wildlife corridors, protected woodland areas, protected sensitive habitat areas with interpretive displays, and other natural areas as meeting the open space or passive parks goal.[32] One way to meet the general plan goal is to supplement the Quimby Act program with a program designed to provide for mitigation of impacts associated with development projects that cause a calculable *loss* of open space. Essentially, while the Quimby Act program requires developers to dedicate land (or pay for) services that will be demanded by new residents, namely, recreational facilities, the new open space conversion program would require payment of impact fees (or dedications of land) to offset the loss of existing community resources, namely, open space, habitat, greenways, riparian areas. Such a program would be structured to implement the "open space element" that is a required part of California general planning.[33] In 2002, the Placer County Planning Department proposed development of an ordinance that would require developers to compensate for certain open space losses associated with development using a formula that would take into account impacts on wildlife habitats, stream habitat, outstanding areas of natural vegetation, and other features. The proposed approach would require an impact fee but would authorize the developer to offer an in-lieu dedication of land (the reverse of the Quimby Act). The Planning Board would consider land based on a number of attributes, including threat, sensitivity, biological values, public access, scarcity, and temporal replacement value.[34] If adopted, the open space conversion program would help mitigate the impact of development on habitat and wildlife.

Placer County is also currently supporting an open space program called Placer Legacy, which acquires lands and easements from willing sellers. Placer Legacy focuses on high quality lands, interconnected open space, and lands and waters that have biological as well as recreational significance. This program currently uses primarily state and local funds including grant funds (about $1.3 million in county funds and $3 million in grant funds), but could be supported in part by the proposed impact fee program.[35]

Subdivision Regulation

Description

Subdivision ordinances govern the conditions under which a single parcel of land may be subdivided into smaller parcels for development and sale. Subdivision ordinances, either together with the zoning ordinance or absent a zoning ordinance in some jurisdictions, define the density of such subdivisions, lot sizes, what requirements apply for streets and utilities and open space, setbacks for buildings, and building dimensions and characteristics. Typically the subdivision ordinance requires the filing of a plat and approval of the plat by the local government. Approval of many subdivisions is "by right" where the provisions of the ordinance have been satisfied. In other instances, often based on the size of the subdivision, the review process is more elaborate.

Subdivision ordinances specify what information must be submitted by the landowner applicant, how the lots must be laid out with reference to buildable and unbuildable areas, and how public utilities and infrastructure will be provided to serve the subdivision. Some jurisdictions provide for "site plan" review in connection with subdivisions to assure that the local government has sufficient opportunity to review the entire plan of development.

Use for Biodiversity

Subdivision ordinances can play an important role in protecting habitats. The ordinance may make certain areas (wetlands, river buffers, etc.) not buildable and may even eliminate these areas from the density calculation for the tracts. Subdivision ordinances may make cluster development mandatory or available by right.

Subdivision regulations relevant to biodiversity protection may define maximum lot sizes to assure a certain density that, when combined with open space requirements, can protect areas of land from development. Lot averaging is another subdivision ordinance technique that allows flexibility in lot size and subdivision design while maintaining a desired density. Under lot averaging, the resulting lots may be different sizes and shapes—thus facilitating the protection of natural features—while maintaining a prescribed average density of development. Such an approach can be used to assist in preserving natural features such as habitat corridors, woodland patches, wetland, and other open spaces. Lot averaging can also be useful in instances where the local government desires that all the lands be subdivided and conveyed and that there be no commonly held open space or residual large tract. The larger lots may contain the areas off limits to building while the density can be maintained by other lots being smaller.

Subdivision ordinances may provide for setbacks of buildings. These setbacks may be ecological as well as lot-line setbacks—for example, requiring that structures be set back from ecologically important features, waterways, etc. Similarly, street width provisions can help address concerns with impervious surfaces, make cluster development possible, facilitate wildlife crossings, and address other conservation concerns. Stormwater management requirements are also often addressed in subdivision regulations; management of water flow and vegetation can be an important contributor to biodiversity conservation.

Subdivision ordinances may require a landowner to submit detailed information on site characteristics, natural resources, and other features important for biodiversity.

Key Biodiversity Elements

Subdivision ordinances can protect biodiversity with consideration of the following key elements:

1. The local government should adopt subdivision ordinances that ensure the efficient use of land—providing for sufficient density of development while conserving open space areas, habitat connections, and other conservation features.

2. The ordinance should require the mapping and identification of natural features identified in the comprehensive plan and zoning ordinance (if any) so that the local government can effectively review the

layout of lots, roads, and buildings with reference to landscape features important for biodiversity.

3. The ordinance should protect ecological features, habitat patches and corridors, and buffers either by defining the configuration of lots containing or affecting such areas so that their fragmentation and development is made less likely, or by excluding such areas from the buildable area.

4. The ordinance should address the location and design of infrastructure with attention to potential impacts on biodiversity, including requirements to make transportation infrastructure and stormwater management compatible with the biodiversity needs of the area.

5. The ordinance may address the timing of construction activities and provide for conditions necessary to protect species' life cycle, breeding, cover, migration, hibernation, or other needs.

6. The ordinance drafters should consider subjecting small subdivisions to review requirements normally reserved by the local government for larger subdivisions when the small subdivisions are located in a conservation overlay zone or an area otherwise identified as ecologically significant.

Subdivision Regulation in Sensitive Areas—Park City, Utah

Park City's Sensitive Area Overlay Zone Regulations have a number of provisions requiring landowners to consider and protect biodiversity in the context of subdivision review. Specifically, under the ordinance an applicant for approval of development (subdivision, building permit, site plan) must produce a sensitive lands analysis that identifies and delineates specific features. The features for which mapping is required include steep slopes, ridge line areas, vegetative cover, wetlands, stream corridors, and wildlife habitat areas. The map of wildlife habitat areas must be accompanied by a wildlife and habitat report, which must describe and define:

(a) The ecological and wildlife use characterization of the property explaining the species of wildlife using the areas, the times or seasons the area is used by those species, and the value, e.g., meaning feeding, watering, cover, nesting, roosting, or perching, that the area provides for such wildlife species;
(b) the existence of wildlife movement corridors;
(c) the existence of special habitat features, including key nesting Sites, feeding areas, calving or production areas, use areas for migrant song birds and grassland birds, fox and coyote dens, deer and elk winter concentration areas as identified by the Utah Division of Wildlife, and areas of high terrestrial or aquatic insect diversity;
(d) areas inhabited by or frequently utilized by any species identified by state or federal agencies as "threatened" or "endangered";
(e) the general ecological functions provided by the site and its features;

(f) potential impacts on these existing wildlife species that would result from the proposed movement.[36]

In addition, in order to "promote, preserve, and enhance wildlife and wildlife habitat areas in and around Park City," all sensitive or specially valued species are protected by specific additional provisions:

(a) Construction shall be organized and timed to minimize disturbance of Sensitive or Specially Valued Species occupying or using on-site and adjacent natural areas.

(b) If the development site contains or is within five hundred feet of a natural area or habitat area, and the wildlife and habitat report show the existence of Sensitive or Specially Valued Species, the development plans shall include provisions to ensure that any habitat contained in any such natural area shall not be disturbed or diminished, and to the maximum extent feasible, such habitat shall be enhanced.

(c) If the development site contains existing natural areas that connect to other off-site natural Areas, to the maximum extent feasible the development plan shall preserve such natural area connections. If natural areas lie adjacent to the development site, but such natural areas are not presently connected across the development site, then the development plan shall, to the extent reasonably feasible, provide such connection. Such connections shall be designed and constructed to allow for the continuance of existing wildlife movement between natural areas and to enhance the opportunity for the establishment of new connections for movement of wildlife.

(d) If wildlife that may create conflicts for future occupants of the development are known to exist in areas adjacent to or on the development site, then the development plan must include provisions to minimize these conflicts to the extent reasonably feasible.[37]

Chapter Five Endnotes

1. BOULDER COUNTY, COLO., LAND USE CODE art. 7, §1700, *available at* http://www. co.boulder.co.us/lu/lucode (last visited Dec. 10, 2003).

2. BELLEVUE, WASH., LAND USE CODE §20.30D.120.

3. *Id.* §20.30D.150.

4. *Id.* §20.50038.

5. *Id.* §20.30D.160.A.

6. *Id.* §20.50038.

7. WASH. REV. CODE §36.70A.060.

8. Telephone Interview with Michael Paine, City of Bellevue (Dec. 4, 2002).

9. Telephone Interview with Michael Paine, City of Bellevue (Jan. 7, 2003).

10. Exactions and impact fees are not authorized in many states or may be limited to specific capital improvements such as roads, e.g., VA. CODE §15.2-2317, authorizing impact fees only for the most populous counties and limiting their use to roads.

11. *See* DAVID L. CALLIES ET AL., BARGAINING FOR DEVELOPMENT: A HANDBOOK ON DEVELOPMENT AGREEMENTS, ANNEXATION AGREEMENTS, LAND DEVELOPMENT CONDITIONS, VESTED RIGHTS AND THE PROVISION OF PUBLIC FACILITIES (Envtl. L. Inst. 2003); *see also* GROWING SMARTER LEGISLATIVE GUIDEBOOK 8-192 to -200 (Stuart Meck ed., American Planning Ass'n 2002) (state legislation on development agreements).

12. *See* Dolan v. City of Tigard, 512 U.S. 374, 24 ELR 21083 (1994). These precise constitutional requirements have not been applied to impact fees nor to proffers. However, impact fees and proffers must bear some rational relationship to the development activity. The New York Court of Appeals recently upheld a town's requirement of an in-lieu fee of $1,500 per subdivided lot to support parkland, finding the relevant nexus and proportionality based on a legislative scheme. Twin Lakes Dev. Corp. v. Town of Monroe, 1 N.Y.3d 98 (N.Y. 2003).

13. Virginia uses the proffer system rather than exactions.

14. LOUDOUN COUNTY, VA., COMPREHENSIVE PLAN 1-1 (2001), *available at* http:// www.co.loudoun.va.us/bos/docs/boscompplanrevi_/generalplan_/index.htm (last visited Dec. 10, 2003) [hereinafter PLAN].

15. *Id.* at 5-23.

16. *Id.* at 5-1. Green infrastructure is a concept that recognizes the important contribution of ecological services—including water quality, open space, and biodiversity—to the support of the human community. *See generally* GreenInfrastructure.net, *at* http://www.greeninfrastructure.net (last visited Dec. 10, 2003).

17. PLAN, *supra* note 14, at 5-4.

18. *Id.* at 5-23.

19. *Id.* at 5-1, 5-27.

20. *Id.* at 5-1.

21. *Id.* at 3-5.

22. *See generally id.* ch. 10.

23. *Id.* at 10-3.

24. Telephone Interview with Van Armstrong, Program Manager, Division of Land Use Review, Loudoun County Planning Department (July 2002).

25. *See generally* PLAN, *supra* note 14, ch. 5.

26. *Id.* at 3-6.

27. *Id.* at 3-5.

28. *Id.* at 1-1.

29. PLACER COUNTY, CAL., GENERAL PLAN §5, *available at* http://www.placer.ca.gov/planning/planning-docs.htm (last visited Dec. 10, 2003).

30. *Id.* §6.

31. CAL. GOVT. CODE §66477, *available at* http://www.leginfo.ca.gov/calaw.html (last visited Dec. 10, 2003).

32. PLACER COUNTY, CAL., GENERAL PLAN §5.

33. CAL. GOVT. CODE §66560(b).

34. Memorandum to Board of Supervisors from Frederic K. Yeager, Director of Planning, on Open Space Conversion Policy (July 12, 2002).

35. Placer County, California, *Placer Legacy Open Space and Agricultural Conservation Program, at* http://www.placer.ca.gov/planning/legacy/legacy.htm (last visited Dec. 10, 2003).

36. PARK CITY, UTAH, MUNICIPAL CORP. MUNICIPAL CODE §15-2.21-3(B)(8).

37. *Id.* §15-2.21-9.

Chapter Six—Growth Management and Infrastructure Ordinances

Over the past 30 years, local governments have developed expertise in applying land use tools beyond traditional planning, zoning, and subdivision rules to influence the pattern of development on the larger landscape, and especially to provide for management of growth. Many of these tools deal with where development is encouraged and supported by public investments in infrastructure and where development is discouraged and open space and environmental resources are to be conserved, supported, and restored. This chapter discusses:

- Transfer of Development Rights (TDRs);
- Purchase of Development Rights (PDRs);
- Urban Growth Boundaries;
- Priority Development Areas/Urban Service Boundaries;
- Adequate Public Facilities Requirements;
- Transportation Strategies; and
- Revitalization Incentives.

TDRs

Description

TDRs programs are used to limit development or development intensity in one area and to concentrate development in another. TDR programs allow the transfer of development potential from land areas the local government designates to protect (sending areas) to areas designated for growth (receiving areas). This requires zoning of both areas to create a market for development rights. Landowners in sending areas, where development is limited or prohibited, can separate their development rights from their "bundle" of property rights to sell to developers for use in receiving areas where development is more suitable. The purchase of TDRs allows a developer in the receiving zone to exceed normal zoning or subdivision limitations on density, height, or other requirements in order to engage in more intensive use of the receiving property. In general, the price of the development rights being transferred is left to the private market, and the local government does not try to affect that price. Local governments may, however, try to facilitate the functioning of a viable market for buyers and sellers of development rights in order to support the achievement of the underlying public goal—a shift in the location and intensity of development from areas less able to support to areas that are intended to do so.

NATURE-FRIENDLY ORDINANCES: LOCAL MEASURES TO CONSERVE BIODIVERSITY

Use for Biodiversity

TDR programs can serve biodiversity objectives by helping to maintain larger areas of contiguous habitat and allowing the functioning of natural disturbance patterns. Such programs have best been used to conserve large areas of ecological significance, ordinarily in conjunction with other strategies. TDR programs are less well-suited for protection of small areas or isolated ecological features as these may not generate enough development rights to support a market for such rights.

TDR programs can protect rare landscape elements, sensitive areas, and associated species if these are located across a readily definable and fairly sizeable area of land. Because of the need for a fairly large area to generate TDRs and enough demand for their use in a receiving area, such programs are seldom useful for biodiversity purposes within a single small municipality. In general they will need to operate at a multimunicipal, county, or even multicounty level.

Key Biodiversity Elements

TDRs can be used for biodiversity conservation by taking into account the following key elements:

1. TDRs are best used when there is a substantial land area to be protected and a practical limit on the amount of developable land otherwise available within the jurisdiction or jurisdictions where the TDRs will be used. Unless there is some demand for the use of TDRs, there will be no purchasers.[1] If a significant amount of easily developable land is widely available in the jurisdiction, a TDR approach may not work well because there will be no advantage to a developer buying additional rights. In designing a TDR system for biodiversity, the jurisdiction should carefully define a substantial land area that contains the ecological features needing protection. The ordinance should be based on information that shows why reduced density is critically important for the areas to be protected. At the same time, the receiving areas should be defined to encompass areas of anticipated high market demand but not showing the biological characteristics of the sending areas.

2. The ordinance should include a thorough and careful definition of the conservation restrictions on land in the sending areas and the remaining uses authorized on the parcels in the sending areas. These restrictions should, where possible, include provisions that allow natural ecological processes to operate (such as flooding, some provision for vegetation life cycles and nutrient cycling, and maintenance of habitat structure). The ordinance may be written to ensure that remaining authorized agriculture and timber uses, for example, do not defeat the habitat goals for which the area was established through overintensity or destruction of habitat. At the same time, however, authorized uses

86

within the sending area shall be as broad and flexible as may be consistent with the conservation goals. A range of remaining economically viable uses in the sending areas may make a TDR program politically acceptable and reduce property rights claims by affected landowners.

3. The ordinance should require recordation of a permanent easement (also known as a conservation restriction in same states) on the sending parcel—not just a regulatory notation that the TDR has been used—in order to enhance enforceability and prevent subsequent degradation of the program.

4. The ordinance should create a program for tracking of results on the ground (not just transactions). The value of the program is in its conservation results and these should be made clear, not only to maintain public support for the program but also so that adjustments can be made if the program is not succeeding in its biodiversity conservation goals.

TDRs—Long Island Pine Barrens, New York

In 1993, the New York State Legislature passed the Long Island Pine Barrens Protection Act to enable multiple municipalities in Suffolk County to conserve key areas facing development pressures. The foremost goals of the Act are the preservation of the Pine Barrens ecology and the protection of groundwater quality. Among the tools created to accomplish these goals is a program of TDRs called the Pine Barrens Credit Program.

Concern for the Long Island Pine Barrens environment took root in the early 1960s, as long-term studies conducted by the Long Island Regional Planning Board raised awareness that the island's main aquifer was fed by water filtered through the Pine Barrens and that preservation of the ecosystem was the only way to ensure continued water quality. In response, Suffolk County began a program of public land acquisition to protect the Pine Barrens. Between 1960 and 1993, approximately 26,000 acres were acquired. This was achieved primarily through direct purchase, and to a smaller extent by offering a tax deduction to owners of landlocked property who donated their land to the county.[2]

In the late 1980s, the U.S. Geological Survey identified Special Groundwater Protection Areas (SGPA), and the planning board conducted water impact studies in nine SGPAs, including the Central Pine Barrens. Concern also began to develop as awareness grew about the special ecological value of the Pine Barrens. The Pine Barrens contains over 300 species of vertebrate animals, 1,000 species of plants, and 10,000 species of insects and other invertebrate animals.[3] The Pine Barrens has unique ecological significance because of its unusually high concentration of endangered species.[4]

In the 1980s, Suffolk County began experiencing great development pressures. At one point in 1989, there were approximately 224 applications for subdivisions in the Pine Barrens. Concerned with the devastating impact that uncontrolled development would have on habitat and water quality, and frustrated by the lack of environmental review and coordination by the towns, the Long Island Pine Barrens Society brought suit against the Town of Brookhaven Planning Board under the State Environmental Quality Review Act (SEQRA), claiming that the town had failed to prepare a cumulative environmental impact statement (EIS) on several of the pending permits.[5] Though the New York State Court of Appeals ruled against the Pine Barrens Society, holding that SEQRA provided no cohesive framework for relating the several projects, the threat of repeated lawsuits worried developers, and the arguments for greater protection got the attention of the state legislature. The legislature decided that it was time for state regulation of Pine Barrens development and convened the stakeholders to negotiate what became the Long Island Pine Barrens Protection Act.[6] Ultimately, the Act involved three towns in the Central Pine Barrens: Brookhaven, Southampton, and Riverhead.

The Act created the Central Pine Barrens Joint Planning and Policy Commission and required the commission to prepare a comprehensive land use plan and generic EIS in order to "preserve the Pine Barrens ecology, and to ensure the high quality of groundwater within the Central Pine Barrens area."[7] The Act articulates five goals: (1) protect, preserve, and enhance the functional integrity of the Pine Barrens ecosystem and the significant natural resources, including plant and animal populations and communities, thereof; (2) protect the quality of surface water and groundwater; (3) discourage piecemeal and scattered development; (4) promote active and passive recreation and environmental educational uses that are consistent with the land use plan; and (5) accommodate development in a manner consistent with the long-term integrity of the Pine Barrens ecosystem and to ensure that the pattern of development is compact, efficient, and orderly.[8]

The Act directed the commission to base the plan on a variety of studies and reports, including: (1) groundwater and ecological studies; (2) general planning studies of human population, commerce, housing, transportation, land use, sites of historical, archeological, or scenic significance, and natural resources, including air, water, open spaces, forests, soils, rivers, wetlands, and other waters, shorelines, fisheries, wildlife, vegetation, threatened species, and minerals; and (3) research on other hydrological or ecological areas analogous to the Central Pine Barrens.[9]

In order to accomplish these goals, the Act divided the nearly 100,000 acres of the Central Pine Barrens into 2 geographic areas: the Core Preservation Area and Compatible Growth Area.[10]

In the Core Preservation Area, the Act requires the plan to: (1) preserve the Pine Barrens in their natural state; (2) promote compatible agricultural, horticultural, and open space recreational uses; (3) prohibit or redirect new construction or development; (4) protect and preserve the quality of surface and groundwaters; and (5) coordinate and provide for the acquisition of private land interests.[11] Development in the Core Preservation Area is not absolutely prohibited, but there is a very heavy burden on the landowner to prove that she or he is entitled to one of the following exceptions: (1) extraordinary hardship; (2) compelling public need based on (a) public health, (b) public water access, or

(c) police access; or (3) agricultural or horticultural use that does not materially alter native vegetation.[12]

In the Compatible Growth Area, the Act requires the plan to: (1) preserve and maintain the essential character of the existing Pine Barrens environment, including plant and animal species and habitats; (2) protect the quality of surface and groundwaters; (3) discourage piecemeal and scattered development; (4) encourage appropriate patterns of compatible development uses in an orderly way while protecting the Pine Barrens from the cumulative adverse impacts thereof; (5) accommodate a portion of development redirected from the preservation area; and (6) allow appropriate growth consistent with the natural resource goals of this article.

The comprehensive land use plan, created by the commission in 1995, identified 55,000 contiguous acres as Core Preservation Area and 47,500 surrounding acres as Compatible Growth Area.[13] These areas were based on biological inventories prepared by the New York natural heritage program, which describes, catalogues, and characterizes New York's biological communities.[14] The boundaries were drawn to incorporate the highest quality ecological sites.

In addition to the Core Preservation Area and the Compatible Growth Areas, there are about 20 pockets in the Compatible Growth Area, called Critical Resource Areas, that were identified by the commission as particularly sensitive or valuable. Though the protection of these areas is not as strong as in the Core Preservation Area (all but four will permit development), developers who wish to build in a Critical Resource Area must demonstrate that they will not disturb the features that caused it to be protected.[15]

By the time the Act was passed, 15,000 acres of the Core Preservation Area had already been developed and 26,000 had been previously acquired by the state and the county. Thus the target became saving 14,000 acres. The Act established two main strategies for achieving that goal: (1) continued public acquisitions, which were to account for 75% of the preservation; and (2) a TDR program.[16]

Under the Pine Barrens Credit Program, owners of land in the Core Preservation Area (sending area) may receive Pine Barrens Credits (PBCs) for the foregone development potential of their property. These credits can then be sold to those who wish to exceed town planning department limits for density or intensity, or county health department limits on nitrate releases in designated "receiving" areas.[17] The allocation of PBCs is based on underlying town zoning law. One credit is allocated for each single-family dwelling permitted on a residentially zoned parcel of land located in the Core Preservation Area. This is based on a development yield table and the zoning regulations in existence in June 1995. For example, if zoning allowed 1 dwelling unit per 10,000 square feet lot area, the development yield factor would be 2.7 PBCs per acre.[18] The greater the previously permitted density, the greater the development yield factor. Thus, sellers get credit by multiplying the gross lot area by the development yield factor for each residential zoning category. Though there are very few parcels in the preservation area that are zoned commercial or industrial that are not already developed that way, credits for nonresidentially zoned land in the Core Preservation Area are awarded at a rate of one credit per acre.[19]

Each of the three affected towns, Southampton, Riverhead, and Brookhaven, is required to identify receiving areas for the development rights that come from Core Preservation Areas within their jurisdiction. First, they must establish "as of right" areas to accept, on a 1:1 ratio, the number of credits that could be sent from their Core Preservation Area. These receiving areas are mapped as Residential Overlay Districts, and developers need not get special approval to use the PBCs in these areas (other than regular zoning requirements). However, in order to prevent harm from increased development in the receiving areas, no receiving area can exceed a 20% density or intensity increase as a result of PBCs.[20]

As a matter of good planning and in order to create a stronger market for the PBCs, the towns are encouraged to plan enough receiving areas to accommodate 2.5 credits for every 1 sending credit created.[21] Once they have designated enough receiving areas to accommodate the credits from the sending areas, the towns may choose to accommodate credits at their own discretion in order to meet the minimum requirement in ways that provide flexibility. For example, the town of Brookhaven uses Planned Development Districts, subject to the approval of the Town Board, to allow for conversion of residential development rights into commercial, industrial, and/or other uses. This increases the number of PBCs being accepted in the town while limiting the final number of residential dwelling units being added.[22]

The Pine Barrens Credit Clearinghouse was created in order to help establish, facilitate, and maintain a market for PBCs. The clearinghouse established the initial value of PBCs by conducting an economic analysis for each of the three towns before the credits were created. The analysis predicted the difference in value of credits in each of several types of areas in each of the towns, e.g., house in a residential area in a school district, based on what a developer would likely pay for the additional value that the credit would lend to the receiving parcel. This was done for each school district in each town, and averages were calculated for each town. The clearinghouse is also a buyer of last resort in order to ensure that the credits have value. But in order to avoid competing with private transactions, they set the price they would pay at 80% of market value. The commission publishes a registry monthly that lists the credits for sale and lets the parties deal privately. Parties have to register the sale with the commission either voluntarily at the time of the sale or when the buyer wants to "cash it in" with the town planning departments or county health department.[23] The current price of the credits is market driven and varies from around $7,500 to $15,000 per credit, with some extremes, e.g., $15,200 for 0.38 credit.[24]

There are three steps that the property owner must follow in order to obtain a PBC certificate. First, the property owner applies for a Letter of Interpretation from the clearinghouse that acts as an official estimate of the number of credits the property owner will receive, based on the formula discussed above. Second, the property owner applies to the clearinghouse for a PBC certificate by submitting a valid Letter of Interpretation, a standard title report, a survey, and a copy of the proposed conservation easement. Third, the property owner must file the easement with the County Clerk and submit a copy to the clearinghouse with proof of filing. The title search will then be updated, and the clearinghouse will issue the PBC certificate.[25]

In the seven years from June 1995 to October 1, 2003, 830.26 credit certificates were conveyed, 180.99 were redeemed,[26] and 470.75 acres were protected.[27] It is difficult to show the impact that the PBC program has had on biodiversity and water quality because the lands protected by the PBC easements are scattered and interspersed with publicly owned lands. However, The Nature Conservancy and the Protected Lands Council are conducting ongoing monitoring of the ecological health of the region, and the New York natural heritage program is in the process of updating its survey, "Ecological Communities of New York State," which contains a description of current Pine Barrens ecology.

The response of those involved in Pine Barrens protection is mixed. Most agree that the PBC program has had modest goals from the beginning and are not surprised at the relatively small amount of land affected by the TDR program thus far. One commission staff member said that developers respond first to market interest in determining where to develop, and that their decisions are not strongly influenced by the availability of credits.[28] Some attribute the modest performance of the program to the fact that PBCs cannot be redeemed outside of the town in which they were created and that the towns have not reached the goal of identifying 2.5 redemption options for every potential credit.[29] Some suggest that they be made transferable across a wider geographic or political landscape, thereby increasing the potential demand.[30]

PDRs

Description

Often, a large obstacle to enacting TDR programs is creating a market for the TDRs. One solution is for local governments themselves to purchase TDRs from landowners in designated areas. PDR programs often back TDR programs in order to assure that development rights have value and to facilitate the assembly and sale of rights to potential users.

Alternatively, local governments sometimes purchase development rights and retire them in order to prevent future development of these areas. PDR programs can be a form of public acquisition of conservation interests in lands important for biodiversity conservation.

Use for Biodiversity

PDR programs, like TDR programs, are especially useful in helping to protect lands within fairly large defined ecological areas that need conservation of contiguous habitat. PDR programs can also aid in conservation of rare landscape elements, sensitive areas, and associated species. These programs can complement TDR programs and are also closely related to the public land and ease-ment acquisition strategies discussed in Chapter Eight.

Key Biodiversity Elements

A PDR program for biodiversity conservation should contain the follow-ing elements:

1. Ideally, the local government should enact a PDR program at a time when development pressures are not so strong as to inflate the value of the development rights, and when the residual uses of the restricted land remain profitable. By "buying low," the government or PDR bank can help optimize the benefit of its conservation investment.

2. The local government should establish criteria for where PDRs will be purchased from landowners within the sending area. These criteria should include identifying conservation priorities, balancing acquisi-tion policy between landowner offers and conservation preferences, and indicating when and whether premium prices or preferences for purchase should apply to key conservation parcels.

3. The ordinance should specify criteria for deciding whether acquired PDRs are to be retired or banked for resale. When PDRs are to be banked, the ordinance should also establish criteria guiding the subse-quent resale to ensure that the development rights are used to facilitate well-designed projects and that they do not undermine the private commercial market for TDR sales, if it exists.

Purchase of Development Rights—City of Virginia Beach, Virginia

The city of Virginia Beach sits along the Atlantic Ocean, below the mouth of the Chesapeake Bay, and stretches south to the North Carolina border. Within the city's borders is an ecologically rich area containing two national wildlife ref-uges, two state parks, thousands of acres of conservation land, and a network of waterways, tidal marshes, and freshwater wetlands.[31] Natural area inventories of the watershed conducted by the Virginia Department of Conservation and Recreation's Division of Natural Heritage have identified these wetlands as critical habitat for rare and endangered plants and animals. At least 46 rare spe-cies have been documented in the southern watershed. The area provides habi-tat for breeding and migratory waterfowl as they travel along the Atlantic Fly-way, as well as a corridor for bear, bobcats, deer, and other animals as they move between the North Landing River and the Back Bay.[32]

The rich ecology is not the only asset of the region. This area also contains some of the commonwealth's richest farmland. Along with tourism and the mil-itary, agriculture stands as one of the three largest industries in Virginia Beach. But the amount of farmland in the city has dwindled. In 1982, there were ap-proximately 51,000 acres of active farmland, while in 1993, there were only 30,000 acres remaining.[33] During the three decades following its incorporation in 1963, the population of Virginia Beach grew from 111,000 to more than 430,000.[34] Along with this increased population came increased development that began to compromise both the ecology and the agricultural heritage of the area.

The City Council adopted the first comprehensive plan in 1979. Confronted with development that was defying the orderly vision of the comprehensive plan, the city established an urban service boundary in 1986 called the "Green Line."[35] This device prohibited city spending on infrastructure beyond the line in an attempt to encourage more compact development and discourage destruction of sensitive ecosystems and valuable farmland. Despite the Green Line, development continued to push south. In the early 1990s, during a biennial review of the comprehensive plan, a coalition of farm and conservation advocates formed to seek more permanent solutions to the continued threat of sprawl.[36] The committee, concluding that agricultural uses of land were culturally, economically, and ecologically preferable to suburban residential development, agreed on a common goal for their project: to promote and enhance agriculture as an important local industry that is part of a diverse local economy.[37] What came of this process was a proposal for an agricultural reserve program under which the city would pay owners of agricultural land to place a permanent easement on their lands to prohibit nonagricultural uses. Advocates for the proposal conducted outreach programs and education for over a year, and on May 9, 1995, the city of Virginia Beach enacted the Agricultural Lands Preservation Ordinance and the Virginia Beach Agricultural Reserve Program (ARP).[38]

The ARP covers nearly 35,000 acres of land in the southern watershed area beyond the Green Line and is identified in the comprehensive plan.[39] The program is designed to provide farmland owners with a financially attractive alternative to selling their land to developers, allow them to stay on their farms by providing continuing income, and protect the ecological, economic, and cultural value of the land. For land that is deemed eligible, the city will purchase, by installments, an easement that prohibits any nonagricultural use of the land in return for the value that the development rights would have fetched in the development market. In addition, small business development, such as a bed and breakfast, is permitted as long as it does not adversely affect the future agricultural potential of the land.[40]

According to staff at the Virginia Beach Department of Agriculture, the ARP has three main goals: (1) to promote and enhance the agriculture economy; (2) to preserve rural cultural heritage; and (3) to conserve and protect environmentally sensitive lands, waters, and other resources.[41] Another goal, and perhaps one of the stronger selling points of the program for city residents, is the cost savings anticipated by avoiding public infrastructure improvements that go along with expanding development.[42]

The ARP is a completely voluntary program. Unless the farmland owner agrees to participate, she or he will continue to be allowed to develop the land under the current zoning laws.[43] However, the program provides a unique benefit in that it allows farmland owners who would prefer to stay on their land the opportunity to do so while receiving a steady stream of income from the city.

In order to be eligible to participate in the program, the property must: (1) be no less than 10 acres in area, or be combined with contiguous property that together equals at least 10 acres; (2) be wholly located within a residential district, an agricultural district, or a preservation district; and (3) be capable of being subdivided or developed for nonagricultural uses without the approval of the city council.[44] This third factor is intended to address the issue of existing zoning and vested rights.

If the property is eligible, the farmland owner can submit an application to the Virginia Beach Agricultural Advisory Commission. Using assessment criteria established by the ordinance, the commission ranks the land for possible development rights acquisition using five criteria. First, the quality of farmland (productivity and capability) constitutes 35% of the points, and takes into consideration: the size of the farm, the quality of the soil, the percentage of cropland in pasture, on-farm agricultural infrastructure and improvements, percentage of farm in high-value crops, and animal units produced. Second, the circumstances supporting agriculture constitute 25% of the points and take into consideration: the number of nonfarm rural residences within one-half mile of the farm, the proximity of the parcel to other farms with agricultural reserve program or other perpetual easements, the proximity to significant or unique agricultural support services, and batch applications with contiguous parcels. Third, the likelihood of conversion to nonfarm use (development pressure) constitutes 20% of the points and takes into consideration: the urgency of circumstances, the farm's suitability for residential conversion, the percentage of the farm offered to the agricultural reserve program, the amount of public road contiguous to the farm, and the aesthetic value of forest on the farm. Fourth, the environmental quality of the farmland constitutes 15% of the points and takes into consideration: the percentage of the farm in upland forest, the proximity to areas identified as having high environmental value, such as state or federal parks, areas within the Back Bay Wildlife Refuge expansion boundary, exemplary wetlands, critical areas and endangered species habitat, and the proximity of the farm to a perennial stream or waterway. The fifth consideration, which constitutes 5% of the points, is the land's proximity to historic, scenic, or cultural features and the frequency of application submission.[45]

If the commission decides that it wants to buy the development rights on the land, an independent appraisal is completed to determine the value of the development rights for the parcel and to support making the owner an offer. Upon agreement, a permanent easement is filed, and the development rights are held in public trust by the city in perpetuity.[46] The farmland owner receives semiannual payments of the interest on the purchase price for 25 years. At the end of the 25 years, the city pays the farmland owner the principal in one lump sum, funded by zero coupon bonds purchased at the time of the execution of the easement.[47] There are several advantages to this installment method of payment. First, the interest payments are exempt from federal, state, and local income taxes. Second, the property owners may be able to defer recognition of capital gains until they receive the principal amount. Third, after one year from closing, the installment-purchase agreement becomes a negotiable instrument, and the property owner may sell his or her interest in it, the land (without the development rights), or both.[48] Finally, because the easement reduces the value of the land, the owner pays lower property taxes and lower estate taxes.

Though the easement is intended to be held in perpetuity, the ordinance does contain a reopener provision. After a minimum of 25 years from the date the easement is recorded, the property owner (or successor-in-interest to the property which is subject to the easement) may petition the city for the opportunity to repurchase the development rights at the then current market value. This is deliberately difficult to do, and requires that: (1) the sale of the development rights be essential to the orderly development and growth of the city; (2) development of the property for nonagricultural uses would not be in conflict with the comprehensive plan then in effect; (3) three-fourths of the City Council votes to approve the repurchase; and (4) the city must replace the sold development rights with the development rights in the ARP zone of the same or greater financial value.[49] The ARP is funded primarily by a 1.5% real property tax, which generates approximately $3.5 million per year.[50]

The ARP set a goal of protecting 20,000 acres in the 35,000-acre eligible zone.[51] The Director of the ARP estimates that the program has already acquired easements on over 6,000 acres of land since the first purchase in 1997 and says that the demand is steady. He cautioned against rapidly purchasing easements under an installment program unless the budget is designed to grow as the payment burden grows. In addition to preserving thousands of acres of ecologically and culturally significant land, the program has been received well by the community. When the advocates for the program were educating the community, they made sure that the citizens of Virginia Beach understood and accepted the additional local taxes that would be required to pay for the program.[52] While the program is aimed at agricultural land, its focus on lands threatened with development and its attention to natural resources and ecological considerations make it beneficial to biodiversity in this rapidly growing Virginia jurisdiction.

Urban Growth Boundaries

Description

An urban growth boundary is a zoning and infrastructure investment technique that defines designated growth areas adjacent to existing centers. Denser development and public investment are limited to areas within the boundary, while development outside the boundary is restricted or limited to much lower density. This technique can be used to control sprawl and to encourage infill (development of vacant lots and rehabilitation or replacement of obsolete buildings) and compact development of urban centers. Urban growth boundaries are used in Oregon and other states, including Tennessee and Colorado, as well as in specific municipalities around the United States. Despite criticism that the boundary can increase housing costs, several well-documented studies have shown that metropolitan areas with comparable growth demand and without urban growth boundaries have experienced similar price trends as those employing such boundaries.[53]

Urban growth boundaries are most effective when they use "carrot and stick" approaches by providing both incentives for development within the boundary and disincentives for development outside it. Public investment and infrastructure provide one clear incentive for development within the boundaries. Localities also often offer streamlined development approval processes within the boundary to provide a further incentive for development to occur within this area.

Use for Biodiversity

By holding growth within specific geographical limits, urban growth boundaries help to preserve undeveloped habitat. This tool is best for avoiding land uses that adversely affect a large regional area. It is generally not targeted enough to meet other biodiversity objectives, such as habitat corridors and protection of rare and sensitive areas. Additional land use tools will be needed to serve these objectives. However, urban growth boundaries can set the regional context for development and conservation that can allow these other tools to be far more effective. In addition, such boundaries can help to define and conserve a regional matrix of lands that can serve as connections between and among core habitat areas that might otherwise be fragmented.

Key Biodiversity Elements

Urban growth boundaries can serve biodiversity objectives by including the following key elements:

1. An urban growth boundary must be based on a well-supported comprehensive plan that takes into account data about projected human population growth, economic development, habitat quality, natural resource spatial distribution, alternative development scenarios, and infrastructure planning. For biodiversity purposes, the plan should reflect available natural heritage information as well as assessments of the likely effects of development on living resources outside the proposed boundary.

2. The comprehensive plan defining an urban growth boundary should contain detailed findings supporting the denial of infrastructure and public services outside the boundary. It should support the use designations and limitations on development in terms of their effects on biodiversity and natural systems as well as in economic and demographic terms.

3. The urban growth boundary ordinance should provide for zoning of areas outside the boundary for uses compatible with the boundary's objectives—including typically low intensity uses like agriculture, forestry, horticulture, some ancillary businesses, and directly related

dwellings. Where development is to be permitted it should be clustered and compatible with the maintenance of the larger open space areas that constitute the bulk of the area outside the boundary. The zoning ordinance should not discourage owners from maintaining land outside the boundary as conservation land, wildlife habitats, wetlands and woodlands, desert and scrubland, and the like. For this reason, agricultural and forest zoning provisions that require minimum annual income from these activities (typical in urban growth boundary ordinances to prevent sham agricultural and forestry uses that are really upscale residential estates), should have exceptions for land subject to dedicated, verifiable conservative uses.

4. If possible, limitations on introductions of invasive exotic species should be part of the zoning regulations applicable outside the boundary, consistent, however, with best agriculture and forestry practices.

5. The local government should consider adopting ordinances like those discussed in Chapter Four (Planning and Zoning) and Chapter Seven (Conservation Practice Ordinances) to conserve biodiversity within the urban growth boundary. Although these areas will be more densely developed, there are typically key riparian corridors, habitat areas, and parklands that can help support urban biodiversity and assure that the urban landscape retains some connections with the protected areas outside the boundary. Urban greenways and waterfronts frequently can be managed with greater attention to biodiversity.

Urban Growth Boundary—Lancaster County, Pennsylvania

Municipal governments around Lancaster, Pennsylvania, the heart of the Amish country farmland region and a magnet for substantial suburban growth, adopted an urban growth boundary beginning in 1993. Because in Pennsylvania it is municipalities rather than counties that set the rules for land use and development, Lancaster County's boundary required the voluntary enactment of consistent zoning ordinances by 23 separate municipalities or adoption of the county's ordinance by the participating municipalities.[54] The boundaries, which surround the city of Lancaster and 12 boroughs, provide for denser development and public infrastructure within the boundary, and less dense development—including agricultural zoning and agricultural preservation—and fewer infrastructure services outside the boundary. Within the boundaries densities are authorized from very urban densities to 1 dwelling per 2 acres in a limited area; outside the boundaries, residential densities range from 1 dwelling per 10 acres to 1 dwelling per 50 acres in some cases.[55]

Over the course of 10 years, 75% of all new homes in Lancaster County have been constructed within the boundary. Although development outside the boundary did not stop, the boundary made it easier to apply agricultural conservation easement programs at less cost and reduced the density of development outside the boundary.[56] The urban growth boundary made it possible to concentrate both development and land conservation programs in complementary fashion. The boundary is keeping farmland in operation, while allowing population growth and development to continue. The benefits to biodiversity are largely incidental to the continuation of farming and related open space preservation. But the avoidance of fragmentation and large-scale regional depletion of resource lands means that the area outside the Lancaster growth boundary has retained much of the natural diversity it has had for the last 300 years of settlement.

From a biological diversity perspective, the boundary has reduced the rate of sprawl and has led to more opportunities for conservation—including the preservation of larger parcels of land. Water quality work sponsored by state and private land conservation organizations is now underway in local watersheds, which will benefit from the lower densities and the increased potential for restoration of aquatic health. Maintaining the land in farming has made it possible to contemplate use of riparian forest buffers and conservation compatible with agriculture.

Priority Development Areas/Urban Service Boundaries

Description

Priority development areas target public infrastructure funding to designated areas and deny public funding outside these areas. This infrastructure management tool, a major feature of Maryland's Smart Growth program, is designed to avoid subsidizing sprawl and to align infrastructure spending with land use planning. A priority development area is an area of future growth designated by a state or local government, within which the government(s) intend to provide public services and infrastructure. Maryland's statewide Smart Growth legislation identified priority development areas in the currently urbanized areas of the state and authorized local governments to identify their own priority development areas based on state criteria. It then provides that state infrastructure funding will be available only within these areas.[57] The approach is intended to assure that state funding does not support or subsidize development in areas where development is less desirable and is incompatible with protection of agriculture, open space, and biological diversity.

The urban service boundary is a similar concept. There the local government identifies areas of future development where it intends to provide future services. The boundary does not prohibit development outside the boundary, but does notify developers that they cannot expect public funding of services in that area. The urban service boundary concept is used in many places, including California, and operates as a planning tool that advises developers where services like water and sewer will be and will not be provided.

Use for Biodiversity

The urban service boundary does not itself protect areas of land, rare landscape elements, or habitat connections. At most, it discourages dense development in designated areas, and when combined with other tools like cluster zoning, agricultural zoning, or public acquisition of conservation easements, it can strongly affect the pattern of development in a metropolitan region. This can make it possible for other, more focused, efforts to conserve biodiversity.

For example, in a fast growing metropolitan area zoning and subdivision controls may not have kept pace with population growth and housing demand. But an urban service boundary can make it more expensive to develop beyond the boundary or may enable municipalities and counties beyond the boundary to maintain a lower density zoning. This, in turn, may allow the development of a conservation lands acquisition plan or the adoption of a regional network of parks and greenways. Agricultural/ranch preservation programs targeted outside the boundary may also be more effective in conserving the land resources important for biodiversity. The biodiversity benefits, however, depend almost entirely on the uses that continue outside the urban service area. These, in turn, depend upon both economics and what land use regulations, if any, apply. The urban service boundary or priority development area affects one element of the development equation—public support of potentially costly infrastructure.

Key Biodiversity Elements

An urban service boundary can strongly serve biodiversity conservation goals if it incorporates key elements:

1. The urban service boundary or priority development area ordinance must be written tightly to define when areas may be placed within or excluded from the service area. If the ordinance is vague or easily allows expansion of the area, it will not constrain development choices and will produce minimal benefits for biodiversity (or other values, for that matter). The ordinance should clearly define why areas are excluded. The area boundary should be adopted only after consideration of defined ecological information, including state natural heritage information.

2. The ordinance must not be set up to fail. The ordinance must allow for sufficient development within the service area, and, if possible, should constrain maneuvers that might undermine the effectiveness of the boundary such as new municipal incorporations and too-simple "by-right" expansions of the service area. Where expansion is readily allowed, the ordinance drafters should provide exceptions to the expansions to protect key ecological landscape areas, sensitive habitats, habitat connections, and the like. The ordinance could require consultation or approval from the state's natural resources or wildlife agency as a further constraint on such expansion.

3. If possible, targeting other forms of state or local funding to lands outside the urban service area can help achieve the desired biodiversity result. For example, public land and easement acquisition funds may be best spent outside the boundary. Not only will land costs likely be lower because of the reduced development potential of the land, but such investments can help protect key landscape elements important to the regional conservation goal.

4. Consider whether the boundary can be developed in collaboration with neighboring jurisdictions. Some urban service boundaries have been undermined by new incorporations and aggressive annexations by communities outside the boundary.

Urban Service/Priority Development Areas—Baltimore County, Maryland

Baltimore County, which surrounds the separate city of Baltimore, has been defining rural and urban boundaries since the early 1960s in order to protect rural land and manage metropolitan development. The 1963 Plan for the Valleys was commissioned by a citizens' group and was later substantially adopted by the county council and incorporated into the county's master plan. The master plan's Urban/Rural Demarcation Lines (URDLs) were drawn in 1967 to protect watersheds, farming, and scenic and open space in the rapidly developing county. The URDLs were based on a growth management study that evaluated land and resource use in the county and historic development patterns.[58] Since then, the county has utilized updated data to rezone some areas, including creating two new resource conservation zones, one of which is based on greenways and wildlife corridors.[59]

The county's URDLs correspond closely with the area in which the city of Baltimore provides services purchased by the county. Therefore, water and sewage services are provided only within the urban zones defined by the URDLs, effectively directing growth and significantly preserving open space and habitat. Presently, 86% of the county's population lives within the urban zones. The rest of the county, approximately two-thirds, is covered with resource conservation (RC) zones. These RC zones encourage the conservation of large areas and include environmental criteria.

Baltimore County's linkage of open space planning, development planning, and infrastructure was reinforced by Maryland's adoption of a package of Smart Growth laws in 1997. A centerpiece of the state program was the state's Priority Funding Areas legislation, which limits most state development and infrastructure funding to areas that are already developed or that local governments designate for development in accordance with criteria.[60] Under this law, priority funding areas include incorporated municipalities, other existing developed communities, industrial areas, and planned growth areas that are specifically designated by counties. Counties may designate areas only if they meet guidelines for permitted residential density, intended use, and availability of plans for water and sewage services.[61] Thus, state infrastructure funds are used to reinforce local growth management decisions, providing financial and infrastructure support for development in designated areas only. At the same time, state Rural Legacy funding for acquisition of conservation lands and open space funding is devoted to areas outside priority funding areas. Baltimore County's URDLs became the basis for the county's designation of priority funding areas.

In implementing its Smart Growth program, Maryland is showcasing Baltimore County's success in managing development and providing for open space and natural resource lands. Baltimore County, for its part, receives state infrastructure and open space funding that supports its established plan for managing growth and conserving watersheds, open space, forests, and wetlands. State agencies and nonprofit organizations have chosen Baltimore County for ecological and resource management studies to determine the extent to which a highly populated metropolitan county can realize habitat and biodiversity benefits.[62]

Adequate Public Facilities Requirements

Description

Concurrency requirements expressly link development approvals to the concurrent or preceding construction of public infrastructure adequate to support the development. Such requirements prevent development from occurring before there are sufficient roads, schools, or other infrastructure in place to support it.[63] Concurrency requirements can result in allowing new subdivisions only where road improvements are already in place or are constructed simultaneously. Similar requirements may place caps on development linked to the timely construction of adequate public school spaces for the additional population.

Level of service requirements rate the capacity of various infrastructure to serve existing and future development (most often measures of congestion and capacity on roads), and link the approval of development to meeting certain standards of service.

Both of these infrastructure management tools relate to the concept of "adequate public facilities." Adequate public facilities requirements are a way of controlling the pace, timing, and financing of growth.[64]

Use for Biodiversity

If development outstrips infrastructure, costly retrofitting will be required. The foreseeable results will be frustration and delays for the community's residents. Concurrency and adequate public facilities requirements can help avoid these problems. However, these infrastructure management tools do not necessarily help with biodiversity conservation. Coordination of growth with infrastructure can continue to support large-scale development of greenfields areas if sufficient infrastructure dollars are available.

And in some perverse applications, such requirements can even lead to a preference for new development in less developed exurban areas because of the easier ability to meet the level of service requirements on less-busy roads.

However, if infrastructure requirements are linked to careful projections of development, as well as evaluation of the *placement* of new infrastructure, they can result in more compact development and make haphazard sprawl development less likely. Biodiversity is likely to be assisted by adequate public facilities requirements where conservation has been incorporated into a comprehensive plan that identifies key habitat areas and connections, evaluates ways to site infrastructure to avoid fragmentation, and provides for open space as part of the required infrastructure.

For example, consider a rapidly developing township on the fringe of a metropolitan area. Good planning practice should militate in favor of identifying road corridors, future needs for schools and fire stations, parkland, and other infrastructure. If these decisions are deferred until after subdivision of thousands of building lots on scattered parcels, it will be difficult to avoid traffic gridlock, overcrowding of schools, and loss of opportunities to identify suitable lands for active recreation and natural areas. Adoption of an adequate public facilities ordinance will assist the township in controlling the rate and direction of new development, identifying and committing adequate funds to serve the development demands for services, and providing for protection of key natural resources as part of the "green infrastructure" of the community.

Key Biodiversity Elements

Public facilities ordinances can support biodiversity conservation with the following key elements:

1. The public facilities ordinance should clearly articulate the basis for the requirement: calculations needed for roads, water, schools, parks, habitats, etc. The ordinance should include provisions requiring the infrastructure to be planned, sited, and constructed so as to avoid impacts on areas important for biodiversity and especially areas and elements identified in the comprehensive plan.

2. The ordinance should require capital improvement planning and regular review of the plan and require periodic evaluation of its performance with respect to actual development experience in the jurisdiction. The ordinance should also provide a means to allocate available development capacity, including due consideration to biodiversity resource lands and reducing impacts on sensitive areas.[65]

3. The local government should consider whether to prepare joint ordinances or enter into intermunicipal agreements with adjacent jurisdictions to address facilities and concurrency issues.

4. The ordinance should define circumstances for exceptions. In some areas, a municipality may want to allow construction of infrastructure

to follow development for reasons of efficiency, timing, or to stage impacts appropriately (so that all construction either occurs together—if that is desirable—or is staggered to mitigate impacts on habitat—if that is warranted). The ordinance should specifically identify the conditions under which exceptions will be made and link these to clear impacts on habitat, ecological communities, and habitat connections. Deferring or staggering construction may be important in order to avoid impacts on natural communities that are experiencing repeated impacts. A science-based approach should be built into the ordinance.

Infrastructure Concurrency—Carroll County, Maryland

Carroll County, an agricultural county experiencing rapid development, adopted a public facilities and concurrency management ordinance in 1998.[66] The ordinance was designed to relate the approval of new development to the availability of adequate public services, including schools, roads, fire and emergency services, police, and water and sewer capacity. The ordinance is linked to the county's six-year capital improvement plan and requires maintenance of a database of development approvals and available capacity. In order to account for changes over time and to adjust policies as needed, the ordinance calls for an annual review and report on concurrency management.

Each year, the county determines the available threshold capacity for new development based on the existing infrastructure and the six-year capital improvement cycle. When a developer submits a development concept plan, the county staff determines whether capacity is projected to remain adequate for the upcoming cycle; if so, the developer receives a "concurrency management certificate and housing allocation and may proceed with recording and development."[67] If capacity is not available or fully available, the county and developer work out a phasing plan and allocation of available capacity, or the project is deferred until capacity is projected to become available.

The concurrency ordinance has helped the county address the need for infrastructure and services but it has not entirely served the needs for which the ordinance was developed. The ordinance excludes consideration of subdivisions of three lots or fewer in agricultural zones, commercial and industrial development, and projects on "local rural roads." In addition, the ordinance does not apply within the county's incorporated municipalities—whose residents use county roads, schools, and other services. As a result, the pipeline of previously recorded subdivisions and exempt subdivisions has exceeded the projected countywide target for the first six-year cycle (resulting in approximately 75% of all building permits issued since adoption of the ordinance not being subject to the ordinance).[68] In order to address these issues the County Board recently adopted an ordinance establishing a 12-month pause in the approval of new concurrency certificates to allow for revision of the ordinance.[69] During this period, the county will be exploring a number of issues including, among others, coordination with municipalities and inclusion of currently exempt subdivisions in the process.

Carroll County's experience shows how difficult concurrency management can be. The ordinance's provision for annual data and linkage to the capital improvements plan makes it possible to make mid-course corrections. Effects on biodiversity cannot be assessed, as the ordinance focuses on traditional infrastructure and services rather than open space or green infrastructure. Some of the current exemptions allow development that may be incompatible with conservation goals to proceed outside the required evaluation of adequate facilities. Nevertheless, connecting development with services does help the county government evaluate the effects of growth and its location. When coupled with other management tools, concurrency requirements may help support conservation objectives addressed primarily by other planning, zoning, and land conservation tools.

Transportation Strategies

Description

Local governments can adopt various strategies to protect critical areas from the potentially devastating impacts of roads on habitat. They can also adopt strategies to protect identified species that are subject to substantial threats due to their inability to cross highways safely. Using biodiversity data, governments can require that roads under the jurisdiction of local governments maintain a certain distance from critical biodiversity areas or require that new roads be built alongside existing transportation corridors rather than through intact farm and forest land in order to minimize additional habitat fragmentation. Road corridor dedications and reservations can also be made using biological information as well as traditional economic and planning information. Where the state has control over the siting of roads, local government ordinances regarding land uses can sometimes influence state plans. Coordination provisions under federal transportation legislation provide that local land use plans should be taken into account in preparing state transportation improvement plans.

Local governments can also adopt various means of managing transportation better in order to minimize additional road construction and improve transportation efficiency. For example, they (or state governments) may adopt "fix-it-first" policies, leading localities first to improve the efficiency of existing roads before building new ones. They may adopt transportation management strategies, such as high occupancy vehicle lanes to increase carpooling; reversible lanes to reduce the amount of right-of-way and reduce capital costs; and other strategies to reduce the demand for additional roads. Local governments can also adopt measures to reduce the adverse impacts of roads such as traffic calming measures, lower speed limits, and interconnected streets to disperse traffic flow. Local governments can provide for alternative transportation choices such as improved public transit systems and the construction and maintenance of paths for pedestrians and cyclists.

Use for Biodiversity

Roads are a major source of habitat fragmentation. They provide paths for the introduction of invasive species and pollutants. They can be virtually impermeable barriers to reptiles and amphibians needing to cross from uplands to wetlands and waterways, as well as presenting fatal hazards to many mammal species. Development activities supported by new and expanded roadways can have substantial effects on biodiversity as well.

It is important for local governments interested in biodiversity to consider: (1) whether a road is desirable; (2) where a road should be sited; (3) how to size the road; (4) how road corridor effects on species will be understood and mitigated; and (5) how to manage construction, operation, and maintenance. For many roads, state governments will have primary authority to address these issues, but even where this is the case, local governments can often make their influence felt through consultation mechanisms. Where local governments have jurisdiction—for example, over county or subdivision roads—they can directly affect these outcomes although often subject to state safety standards and requirements.

Local governments can adopt standards that require the consideration of habitat elements and evaluate the ecological consequences of road siting. They can adopt construction timing and practice requirements and mitigation provisions to assure that harms are limited to those that cannot reasonably be avoided. Local governments can conduct their own infrastructure planning with greater reliance on biological information and thus avoid habitat fragmentation, introduction of pollutants to waterways, and other adverse consequences of road and bicycle trail construction that is based solely on engineering and level of service considerations.

Municipalities can site roads to avoid critical natural areas and to promote habitat connectivity. By avoiding building more roads, municipalities can limit some of the direction and rate of sprawl, encourage more compact development, avoid destroying natural and agricultural areas, and avoid fragmentation, thereby preserving larger open spaces for biodiversity. And construction specifications can make roads and paths more biodiversity-friendly.[70] A transportation ordinance or provisions in the subdivision ordinance and capital improvements plan can improve biodiversity outcomes under all eight of the conservation guidelines discussed in Chapter Two.

Key Biodiversity Elements

Transportation programs can incorporate biodiversity conservation by incorporating the following key elements:

1. The municipality should explicitly include biodiversity in its required evaluation of proposed transportation projects, including in its capital improvements plan, corridor identification program, and its subdivision requirements.

2. By ordinance the municipality should adopt a policy of avoiding fragmentation of habitat/farmland/open space wherever possible, consistent with meeting its other transportation objectives. To this end, the ordinance could establish a preference for using routes at or near existing transportation corridors and for retrofits and upgrades.

3. The municipality should adopt an ordinance recognizing and promoting multiple modes of transportation—including trails, bicycle paths, and other modes that can improve commuting, inter-neighborhood travel, and safe walks to school. These should be integrated with ecological features identified in the comprehensive plan.

4. The municipality should consider adopting a policy of "fix-it-first" to encourage upgrades and maintenance of existing corridors and infrastructure in preference to new corridors and bypasses that may increase fragmentation.

5. The municipality should adopt an ordinance that, within the municipality's authority, identifies what mitigation measures are needed to deal with road impacts, including issues of construction timing, wildlife crossings and underpasses, and compensatory activities for unavoidable impacts. The state will have primary jurisdiction over many of these activities, but municipal governments have applied requirements to town roads, county roads, and subdivision roads that have resulted in changes in construction practices, timing of excavation, and other measures.

Transportation Strategies—Monroe County, Florida

The Florida Key deer is an endangered species located in an area subject to substantial development pressures. The pressures of development have isolated the estimated 600-800 key deer living on Big Pine Island and No Name Key in Monroe County, Florida, to a six-square mile area. Between 1970 and 1992, 526 road kills of key deer were recorded along U.S. Highway Route 1. In the last decade, key deer road kills have generally exceeded 30 per year.[71]

Since 1995, the Monroe County comprehensive plan, which adopted a state-mandated "level of service" concurrency requirement, has effectively placed a building moratorium on all development on Big Pine Island. While this has prevented additional development, it has not reduced the mortality of key deer due to collisions on U.S. Highway Route 1. In an attempt to protect the endangered key deer, the Florida Department of Transportation (DOT) designed and implemented a wildlife mitigation project in Monroe County addressing 1.5 miles of the 3.1 miles of road that stretch across Big Pine Island through the National Key Deer Refuge.[72]

The Florida DOT is building two highway underpasses that are 25 feet wide and 8 feet high to allow key deer to cross beneath the highway safely. The DOT is also placing cattle guards on access roads (which will discourage deer from entering the highway via these roads). The road itself is not being rebuilt and there are no plans to change its capacity and size. Decisions on the underpass locations were based on the density of the deer and the locations of highest mortality. The U.S. Fish and Wildlife Service helped choose the location and design of the underpasses, employing key deer specialists. When designing the project, the Florida DOT also considered the habitat and population of the endangered lower keys marsh rabbit, which also has been adversely affected by road mortality.

In designing the project, the DOT held stakeholder meetings and involved numerous local and federal agencies and formed the Key Deer Ad Hoc Committee. The DOT experienced opposition from the Key Deer Protection Alliance, which challenged the construction permits for the project. The alliance requested that conditions be placed on the permit such that plans would be altered if the cattle guards failed to protect the deer. The project is funded by a federal wildlife crossing program and by the state. While the project is being carried out by a state agency with jurisdiction, local governments have similar abilities to address roads over which they have jurisdiction, as well as to seek state and federal support for such projects.[73]

Revitalization Incentives

Description

State and local governments provide incentives to encourage infill development and redevelopment of older urban and suburban neighborhoods and commercial districts. The incentives can include such things as tax increment financing (TIF), which dedicates all or a portion of the taxes resulting from the increased value of the revitalized property to the provision of infrastructure and services to support the property itself. The TIF applies within a designated district and only for a defined number of years (often 10-20), after which the taxes are paid as usual to the general treasury of the municipality or school district. Another technique includes tax credits and tax abatements for rehabilitation of older structures (including but not necessarily limited to historic structures). Yet another approach is the provision of "Smart Codes" such as those in New Jersey and Maryland that allow revitalization and reuse of older buildings in urban areas without requiring that the rehabilitated structure meet all the same building codes as a new building. Other programs encourage the reuse of abandoned or underutilized industrial properties. Such "brownfields" programs provide modified cleanup standards and long-term institutional controls, as well as some economic incentives, to ensure that these industrial sites are restored to productive private or public use while limiting human exposure to remaining contaminants.

NATURE-FRIENDLY ORDINANCES: LOCAL MEASURES TO CONSERVE BIODIVERSITY

Use for Biodiversity

Revitalization of existing developed areas, industrial sites, and neighborhoods is an important method for controlling sprawl, reviving economic activity, and restoring local tax bases. Local government actions encouraging such reinvestment have an indirect beneficial impact on biodiversity by ensuring that not all new development occurs in open space (greenfields) areas. Moreover, successful reuse and revitalization policies produce synergistic effects by encouraging more private reinvestment in nearby developed areas, again providing an alternative to sprawl.

In addition to these indirect effects, reuse and revitalization programs can themselves include elements that support biodiversity conservation. For example, Virginia state law specifically provides in its law authorizing the use of tax increment financing for redevelopment projects to include open space as an eligible part of the project.[74] Many older industrial sites and attractive infill sites are along waterfronts and provide excellent sites for at least partial restoration of native plants and functional riparian corridors. Passive recreation, park land, and wildlife areas are often in short supply in older urbanized areas, so these reinvestments can have an important localized effect on urban biodiversity and can also help provide habitat linkages that have long been missing or impaired.

Key Biodiversity Elements

Revitalization incentives can support biodiversity if they include number of key elements:

1. Municipalities adopting revitalization incentives should prohibit use of these incentives to convert greenfields areas to developed uses. The ordinance might allow some small portions of essential land adjacent to the redevelopment area to be included, but only with provisions for required findings, offsets, and mitigation.[75]

2. The ordinance should incorporate biodiversity elements where possible, namely, no fencing or biofriendly fencing, provision for open space, required pervious surfaces, stormwater management using habitat-friendly techniques, habitat restoration, prohibitions on introductions of invasive plants, etc.

Revitalization Incentives—Ford City, Pennsylvania

Brownfields and revitalization incentives can be used to support biodiversity. Pennsylvania has a significant brownfields redevelopment effort called the Land Recycling program.[76] This program, which provides alternative cleanup standards for brownfields areas, has been used in some municipalities to include habitat restoration and enhancement along with redevelopment. One aspect of the program relevant to allowable reuses is an ecological screening process. This requires the landowner to examine a number of issues relevant to biodiversity on reused industrial sites, including pathways of contamination and exposure, species of concern, and habitats of concern. Ecological screening is only required at sites exceeding a minimum size, and the site can be excluded from further screening if it can be demonstrated that pathways of contamination have been eliminated.

Pennsylvania's Land Recycling program also has recently been informally coupled with a "Green Opportunities for Brownfields" initiative, intended to link brownfields uses with potential greenways, recreation areas, and watershed protection. The goal of the initiative is to build more sustainable communities by promoting mixed use land development and incorporating greenways.[77]

In Ford City, an older industrial town, a 43-acre former glass manufacturing facility is being revitalized as commercial property. In connection with the commercial revitalization project, PPG Industries (the landowner and former operator of the plant) agreed to revitalize a former sand quarry and waste slurry lagoon across the Allegheny River from the glass plant as a 90-acre riverview park and nature area.[78] The company agreed to apply phytoremediation technology to reduce pollution runoff and to landscape the area to support active developed recreation on 9 acres and wildlife habitat and viewing on 81 acres suitable for wildlife but not suitable for active recreation.[79] The site managers have purchased and planted native plants and more than 8,000 trees to create the park's wildlife habitat. The enhanced habitat will include native shrubs and trees; warm-season grasslands and wild flowers for ground-nesting birds and pollinators; 34 bird boxes for multiple bird species (including screech owls, kestrels, tree swallowers, and eastern bluebirds); hibernaculum for amphibians; and the preservation of the Glade Run wetland.[80] The habitat enhancement project is a collaborative effort between North Buffalo Township, PPG Industries, the nonprofit Wildlife Habitat Council (a national association of corporate landowners interest in management of corporate lands for wildlife benefit), and various local groups and organizations. The 90-acre parcel will include walking and biking paths and informational signs and lookout platforms.

––––––

The growth management and infrastructure tools discussed in this chapter and the planning and zoning and site development tools discussed in the previous chapters all provide ways to influence the timing and siting of development and land conservation. Local governments also have additional powers to address specific environmental concerns on a jurisdictionwide basis. The next chapter discusses how police-power ordinances can be used independently or in conjunction with zoning and subdivision controls to protect waterways, slopes, vegetation, and other habitat components.

Chapter Six Endnotes

1. A locality can boost the market for TDRs by establishing rules that make it more diffi-cult for developers to obtain approval for higher density development in the receiving areas through any other method. Alternatively, a local government can itself purchase TDRs and create a development rights "bank" or retire purchased rights to prevent their future use. *See infra* section entitled PDRs.

2. Telephone Interview with Lee Koppleman, Director, Center for Regional Policy Studies (July 2002) [hereinafter Koppleman Interview].

3. *See* N.Y. COMP. CODES R. & REGS. §6-182.6.

4. *See* 16 U.S.C. §1531, ELR STAT. ESA §2. *See also* N.Y. ENVTL. CONS. LAW §11-0535; N.Y. COMP. CODES R. & REGS. §6-182.

5. *See* Long Island Pine Barrens Society v. Planning Bd. of the Town of Brookhaven, 591 N.Y.S.2d 982, 986 (1992).

6. Koppleman Interview, *supra* note 2; Telephone Interview with Ray Corwin, Executive Director, Long Island Central Pine Barrens Commission (July 2002) [hereinafter Corwin Interview]; Telephone Interview with John Turner, Director of Conservation Programs, Long Island Chapter, The Nature Conservancy (July 2002) [hereinafter Turner Interview].

7. N.Y. ENVTL. CONSERV. LAW. §57-0121(1).

8. *Id.* §57-0121(2).

9. *Id.* §57-0121(5).

10. *Id.* §57-0121(3)-(4).

11. *Id.* §57-0121(3).

12. *Id.* §57-0121(10).

13. Corwin Interview, *supra* note 6.

14. Turner Interview, *supra* note 6.

15. Corwin Interview, *supra* note 6.

16. Turner Interview, *supra* note 6.

17. Corwin Interview, *supra* note 6.

18. LONG ISLAND CENTRAL PINE BARRENS COMMISSION, CENTRAL PINE BARRENS PLAN ch. 6 (adopted 1995), *available at* http://pb.state.ny.us/cpb_plan/chapter_6.htm (last visited Dec. 11, 2003) [hereinafter CENTRAL PINE BARRENS PLAN].

19. Corwin Interview, *supra* note 6.

20. *Id.*

21. Turner Interview, *supra* note 6.

22. CENTRAL PINE BARRENS PLAN, *supra* note 18, ch. 6.

23. Corwin Interview, *supra* note 6.

24. Long Island Pine Barrens Clearinghouse, *Pine Barrens Credit Certificates Conveyed*, *at* http://pb.state.ny.us/pbc/pbc_certs_conveyed.htm (last visited Dec. 11, 2003).

25. PINE BARRENS CREDIT PROGRAM HANDBOOK: A USER'S GUIDE TO THE CENTRAL PINE BARRENS TRANSFERABLE DEVELOPMENT RIGHTS PROGRAM (1995), *available at* http://pb.state.ny.us/pbc/pbc_handbook.htm (last visited Dec. 11, 2003).

26. Long Island Pine Barrens Clearinghouse, *Pine Barrens Credit Certificates Redeemed, at* http://pb.state.ny.us/pbc/pbc_certs_redeemed.htm (last visited Dec. 11, 2003).

27. Long Island Pine Barrens Clearinghouse, *Pine Barrens Acres Protected, at* http://pb.state.ny.us/pbc/pbc_parcels.htm (last visited Dec. 11, 2003).

28. Corwin Interview, *supra* note 6.

29. Turner Interview, *supra* note 6.

30. Koppleman Interview, *supra* note 2; Turner Interview, *supra* note 6.

31. SOUTHERN WATERSHEDS COMMITTEE, VIRGINIA BEACH AGRICULTURAL RESERVE PROGRAM: A PROPOSAL FOR SAFEGUARDING VIRGINIA BEACH'S PRIME AGRICULTURAL LANDS IN THE SOUTHERN WATERSHEDS i (1994).

32. Telephone Interview with Melvin Atkinson, Agricultural Reserve Program Coordinator, Virginia Beach Department of Agriculture (July 3, 2002) [hereinafter Atkinson Interview].

33. CITY OF.VIRGINIA BEACH, VA., AGRICULTURAL LANDS PRESERVATION ORDINANCE, Ord. No. 2701, §3 (adopted 1995).

34. MARY M. HEINRICHT, FORMING A PARTNERSHIP TO PRESERVE RESOURCES: THE VIRGINIA BEACH AGRICULTURAL RESERVE PROGRAM 2 (1996).

35. Urban service boundaries are discussed *infra* notes 57-69 and accompanying text.

36. Atkinson Interview, *supra* note 32.

37. HEINRICHT, *supra* note 34, at 4.

38. Atkinson Interview, *supra* note 32.

39. *Id.*

40. HEINRICHT, *supra* note 34, at 21.

41. Atkinson Interview, *supra* note 32.

42. *See supra* note 33, §2.

43. Virginia Beach Agriculture, *Agricultural Reserve Program, at* http://www.vbgov.com/dept/agriculture/arpeligible.asp (last visited Dec. 11, 2003).

44. *See supra* note 33, §7.

45. *Id.* §12.

46. SOUTHERN WATERSHEDS COMMITTEE, *supra* note 31, at v.

47. Atkinson Interview, *supra* note 32.

48. Virginia Beach Agriculture, *Agricultural Reserve Program—Advantages to Owners, at* http://www.vbgov.com/dept/agriculture/arpadvantage.asp (last visited Dec. 11, 2003).

49. *See supra* note 33, §11.

50. Atkinson Interview, *supra* note 32.

51. *Id.*

52. HEINRICHT, *supra* note 34, at 6.

53. J. Phillips & E. Goodstein, *Growth Management and Housing Prices: The Case of Portland, Oregon,* 18 CONTEMP. ECON. POL'Y 334-44 (2000); Michael Lewyn, *Oregon's Growth Boundaries: Myth and Reality,* 32 ELR 10160 (Feb. 2002).

54. Tom Daniels, *Farm Follows Function,* PLAN., Jan. 2000.

55. Christian D. Berg, *Urban Growth Boundaries Help Provide Certainties*, ALLENTOWN MORNING CALL, Mar. 7, 1999.

56. Ryan Robinson, *A Limited Success*, LANCASTER NEW ERA, Dec. 9, 2002.

57. MD. CODE ANN. STATE FIN. & PROC. §§5-7B-01 et seq.

58. Baltimore County, Maryland, *History of Master Planning, at* http://www.co.ba.md.us/Agencies/planning/master%20planning/masterplan_history.html (last visited Dec. 11, 2003).

59. Telephone Interview with Don Outen, Baltimore County (Aug. 22, 2002) [hereinafter Outen Interview].

60. *See supra* note 57.

61. Maryland Department of Planning, *Smart Growth Priority Funding Areas Act of 1997, at* http://www.mdp.state.md.us/fundingact.htm (last visited Dec. 31, 2003).

62. Outen Interview, *supra* note 59.

63. Linking development to availability of public infrastructure was upheld in *Golden v. Planning Bd. of the Town of Ramapo*, 285 N.E.2d 291, 2 ELR 20296 (N.Y. 1972).

64. FLA. STAT. chs. 163.3161, 163.3180 (Florida's adequate public facilities requirements).

65. *See* GROWING SMART LEGISLATIVE GUIDEBOOK 8-173 (Stuart Meck ed., 2002) (adequate public facilities ordinance considerations).

66. CARROLL COUNTY, MD., ORD. 161 (Mar. 5, 1998).

67. CARROLL COUNTY, MD., CODE ch. 167, §167-1, *available at* http://ccgov.carr.org (last visited Dec. 11, 2003).

68. CARROLL COUNTY DEP'T OF PLANNING, SPECIAL REPORT TO THE BOARD OF CARROLL COUNTY COMMISSIONERS (2003), *available at* http://ccgov.carr.org/plan-d/deferral/index.html (last visited Dec. 11, 2003).

69. ZONING TEXT AMENDMENT, DEFERRAL ORDINANCE, CARROLL COUNTY, MD., Ord. No. 03-09 (2003).

70. *See generally* RICHARD T.T. FOREMAN ET AL., ROAD ECOLOGY: SCIENCE AND SOLUTIONS (Island Press 2002) (comprehensive coverage of ecological issues and conservation, planning, construction, and maintenance approaches tried in various jurisdictions and ecological settings). *See also* Federal Highway Administration, *Keeping It Simple: Easy Ways to Help Wildlife Along Roads, at* http://www.fhwa.dot.gov/environment/wildlifeprotection (last visited Dec. 31, 2003).

71. Telephone Interview with Cathy Owen, Florida Dep't of Transportation (Aug. 5, 2002); Mick Putney, Key Deer Protection Alliance (Aug. 20, 2002).

72. CATHERINE B. OWEN, FLORIDA DEPARTMENT OF TRANSPORTATION, SR5/US-1 KEY DEER MOTORIST/CONFLICT STUDY, BIG PINE KEY, MONROE COUNTY, FLA. (2002).

73. Federal Highway Administration, *Critter Crossings: Linking Habitats and Reducing Roadkill, at* http://www.fhwa.dot.gov/environment/wildlifecrossings/main.htm (last visited Dec. 11, 2003).

74. VA. CODE ANN. §58.1-3245.1.

75. The American Planning Association's *Growing Smart Legislative Guidebook* model provisions for redevelopment areas prohibits the net loss of "greenfield areas" except for de minimis losses. GROWING SMART LEGISLATIVE GUIDEBOOK, *supra* note 65, §14-301.

76. Land Recycling and Environmental Remediation Standards Act (Act 2), 35 P.S. §§6026.101-6026.908.

77. Pennsylvania Dep't of Environmental Protection, *Green Opportunities for Brownfields: Conservation Planning for Recycling Land*, *at* http://www.dep.state.pa.us/dep/deputate/airwaste/wm/LANDRECY/facts/green.htm (last visited Dec. 11, 2003).

78. Telephone Interview with Rick Jacobs, PPG Industries (Jan. 3, 2003).

79. Telephone Interview with Jon Matviya, Pennsylvania Dep't of Environmental Protection, Southwest Regional Office (Nov. 27, 2002).

80. Ford City Lagoon Project "Scripps' Pond"—A Proposal for Development of a Nature Reclamation/Recreational Area in North Buffalo Township, Pennsylvania, PowerPoint Presentation by a Consortium Organized by Ford City (2002) (on file with author).

Chapter Seven—Conservation Practice Ordinances

Many local ordinances deal with specific conservation concerns. These ordinances frequently apply jurisdictionwide and can be quite useful, if properly designed, in protecting and restoring local biodiversity. This chapter covers:

- Floodplain Management;
- Wetlands and Watercourses;
- Stormwater Management/Sediment and Erosion Control;
- Steep Slope Limitations;
- Forest Conservation/Tree Protection;
- Vegetation Controls; and
- Utility Right-of-Way Siting and Management

Floodplain Management

Description

Floodplain protection ordinances directly regulate development activities in and around floodplains. These ordinances typically are aimed primarily at preventing damage to structures and loss of life due to severe weather events, but they can also be used to protect sensitive riparian habitat and wetlands found in the floodplain. Floodplain protection ordinances generally establish buffer zones around watercourses and their associated floodplains, limiting development activities in these areas and encouraging restoration of riparian wetlands and forested buffers. In addition, where natural drainage systems have already been impeded by development, these ordinances can create alternative drainage facilities. Thus, these ordinances can help to protect the integrity of the floodplain ecosystem and ensure that floodplains remain capable of handling severe weather events without major damage to the ecosystem or built infrastructure. Floodplain ordinances can promote the restoration and maintenance of natural vegetation, wetlands, wildlife corridors, and other features important to biodiversity.

Use for Biodiversity

Floodplains serve numerous ecological functions. They are themselves large contiguous areas of habitat, often containing unique assemblages of water-dependent plants and animals. Flooding is one of those natural patterns of disturbance that serves to replenish nutrients, assure ecological succession, and maintain resilience of the habitat. The floodplain also serves as an im-

115

portant connector of habitat areas and a transition zone between upland and aquatic habitats.

Floodplain ordinances can help assure that development and paving do not impair portions of the floodplain nearest to the waterway. Indeed, many ordinances preserve much of the floodplain and provide opportunities for ecological restoration. Such ordinances prohibit or limit development within the floodplain or some portion of the floodplain. Some ordinances count the floodplain as part of mandatory open space requirements in zoning and subdivision ordinances. Some ordinances provide for mandatory cluster development in areas that include floodplains. Others provide for mandatory setbacks and require vegetated buffers between developments and the waterway.

All of these provisions can generally be justified on safety grounds and prevention of flood damage, but they also serve substantial biodiversity objectives.

Key Biodiversity Elements

A floodplain ordinance can be tailored to protect and conserve biodiversity and ecological functions in the floodplain if it contains the following elements:

1. The ordinance should address safety and flood hazard issues but should also explicitly state the importance of maintaining a biologically functional floodplain. Thus, it will include language identifying the flood control and pollution control effects of a healthy and biologically functioning riparian system. Such language will enable the specific requirements of the ordinance to rely on biological considerations (such as wetland vegetation, infiltration and uptake capacity of soils and biomass), as well as engineering considerations (such as area of the floodway, dimensions of flowage easements).

2. The ordinance should define a specific vegetated buffer area within which no permanent structures are authorized (or define which structures are authorized by permit). The buffer areas should be determined by the local government based on ecological information including natural heritage information and scientific recommendation.[1]

3. The ordinance drafters should consider whether to require dedication of conservation easements within the floodplain in order to ensure long-term enforceability and to maintain the function of the floodplain.

4. Ordinance drafters should consider specifying retention of trees and/or a percentage of land to be covered by certain types of vegetation within the buffer area.

5. The ordinance should provide for mitigation of unavoidable impairments to the floodplain, such as requiring restoration activities to offset structures that constrain flowage.

6. Local government planners should consider whether to direct miti-

gation or open space offsets required from development of areas outside the floodplain into the floodplain. Such a strategy could achieve more conservation and restoration of floodplain habitat, thus supporting key biodiversity connections beneficial to the jurisdiction at large.

Floodplain Management—Howard County, Maryland

Howard County, Maryland, lies within the watersheds of the Patuxent and the Patapsco Rivers in the Chesapeake Bay watershed. The state's 1992 Planning Act requires that all county and local governments include in their comprehensive plans a Sensitive Areas component that protects streams and buffers, 100-year floodplains, steep slopes, and habitats for threatened and endangered species.[2] Howard County has done so. It also adopted specific floodplain preservation regulations as a part of its regulations for subdivision of land.

Howard County does not rely solely on regulatory prohibitions and limitations to address floodplain lands. Most land within the 100-year floodplain in Howard County is designated in the county's General Plan for conservation status, in the county's parks master plan for potential acquisition as a conservation area, or in the county's capital improvement program for potential acquisition as a conservation area. The subdivision regulations state that "developers are encouraged to dedicate and deed the land in the 100-year floodplain to Howard County as permanent open space."[3] Otherwise, the regulations provide, the developer is required to grant the county a perpetual easement for access and either deed the floodplain land to a property owners' association or include it within the boundaries of the individual subdivision lots. The owner of the floodplain land may use the area in any manner consistent with the maintenance and preservation of the area as a floodplain and consistent with the easement. However, the floodplain land is not counted as meeting any part of the requirement for minimum lot size (with limited exceptions in certain rural districts). On final plats and site development plans, floodplain limits must be clearly defined and show floodplain elevations, bearings and distances or coordinated values, and shall be labeled as "100-year floodplain, drainage, and utility easement."[4]

The regulations prohibit developers from storing or discarding building materials and other debris in floodplains. They prohibit any clearing, excavating, filling, altering drainage, impervious paving, or placement of structures except in limited circumstances where required or authorized by the county's Department of Planning and Zoning subject to the advice of specified county and state agencies.

Supplementing the floodplain regulations, the county also prohibits grading, removal of vegetative cover and trees, paving, and new structures within 25 feet of any wetland, within 50 feet of an intermittent streambank, within 75-100 feet of any perennial streambank in residential zoning districts, and within 50 feet of a perennial streambank in nonresidential zoning districts.[5]

The county's General Plan, as revised in 2000, provides for additional, focused watershed planning and management. It notes that "watershed-based plans . . . provide a framework to address other resource issues such as forest and wildlife habitat protection and creation in an integrated, comprehensive manner."[6] The General Plan calls for restoration of degraded or threatened areas along streams as a prime element of community planning efforts.[7]

Wetlands and Watercourses

Description

Local wetlands protection ordinances protect wetlands by regulating development activities in wetland areas and their surrounding buffer zones. They can require, for example, design review, review of grading and building permits, limitations on certain activities, e.g., operation of motorized vehicles, filling, dumping, grazing, limitations on pesticide use, and prohibition of soil disturbances (including grading, plowing, and cultivating). In addition, wetland protection ordinances can require the implementation of stormwater management plans or floodplain management plans to protect wetlands from excessive runoff and nonpoint source pollution.

As authorized by state law or under home-rule authority, local wetland protection ordinances can also impose mitigation requirements for authorized impacts to wetlands. Therefore, even if the ordinance generally prohibits the destruction of wetlands, in cases where impacts are authorized, it can require mitigation. Mitigation can take the form of minimizing the impact by limiting the magnitude or degree of the action; repairing, rehabilitating, or restoring the affected wetland environment; reducing or eliminating the impact over time; or compensating for the impact by replacing, restoring, or providing for conservation of substitute wetland areas.

Local governments can also protect wetlands through the planning and regulation of infrastructure projects. For example, they may condition local approval of sewage facilities on wetland protection activities, or condition funding of public works projects on the project's consistency with state and local wetland protection policies.

Use for Biodiversity

Wetlands and watercourses ordinances can protect substantial biological communities and ecological functions. Protection of these areas meets the conservation guidelines of protecting rare landscape elements, sensitive areas, and associated species. These landscape features can also serve as important habitat corridors. Wetlands and watercourses ordinances can also limit the dispersal of pollutants and promote the continued operation of natural processes such as flooding and nutrient exchange.

Typical requirements will establish no-build buffer areas, vegetation retention requirements, limitations on impervious surfaces, some density limitation, and other provisions tied to the functioning of the wetland or watercourse. *See* Figure 5.

Figure 5: Wetlands and Watercourses Buffer

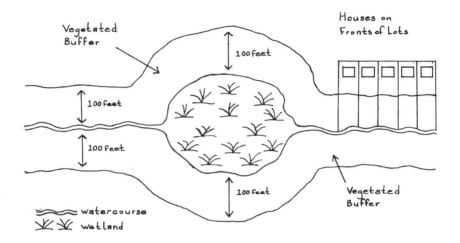

Drawing by Kathryn Hubler

NATURE-FRIENDLY ORDINANCES: LOCAL MEASURES TO CONSERVE BIODIVERSITY

Key Biodiversity Elements

Wetlands and watercourse ordinances can be made supportive of biodiversity with the following key elements:

1. The ordinance should be tied to relevant scientific buffer zone standards suitable for *both* habitat and water quality. Be careful to determine the derivation of routine buffer prescriptions, e.g., 50 feet, 100 feet, 300 feet. Some of these are based on water quality concerns, others on ecological requirements. Still others are compromise standards that protect neither habitat nor water quality. The local government may use state standards if available and absent any more closely tailored local standards.

2. The local government should consider linking its watercourses plan to a larger regional plan for waterways, greenways, and protected areas, if such a plan exists. At a minimum, the plan should be prepared in consultation with advice from the state's natural heritage program.

3. The ordinance should define a buffer area within which building is prohibited. Such a buffer should be wider in steep slope areas.

4. The ordinance should define vegetation retention requirements and/or replacement requirements.

5. Ordinance drafters should consider regulating lighting, and especially outdoor lighting, in the vicinity of the wetland or watercourse. This can be critically important to conserve habitat functions for wildlife, particularly for amphibians, reptiles, and terrestrial animals that may use the watercourse or wetland as a corridor, or for breeding and cover.

Wetland Protection—Village of Schaumburg, Illinois

The village of Schaumburg, Illinois, adopted a wetland protection overlay district as an amendment to its zoning ordinance.[8] The purposes of the district are defined as protecting people and property "within and adjacent to wetlands from potentially hazardous geological and hydrological conditions; prevent[ing] environmental degradation of the land and water; and ensur[ing] that development enhances rather than detracts from or ignores the natural topography, resources, amenities, and fragile environment of wetlands within the village."[9]

Under the ordinance, all plans for development adjacent to or within identified wetlands in the overlay district must fit the topography, soils, geology, hydrology, and other conditions existing on the proposed site. The development must be designed and laid out to keep grading, excavation, landscaping, and other site preparation to an "absolute minimum impact" on the wetlands area. The development must minimize disruption of existing land and animal life,

120

minimize disruption of natural drainage ways, be timed so as to minimize impact on wetlands areas, blend landscaped areas with natural landscapes, and demonstrate a concern for the view of and from wetland areas.[10]

The areas protected by the district are those immediately adjacent to or within wetlands as mapped in the wetlands protection district map included in the ordinance. The ordinance imposes specific restrictions, requirements, and standards within designated wetlands areas. With the exception of approved drainage structures and open space and recreation space uses that do not involve destruction of vegetation or alter natural drainage ways, development is prohibited unless the village approves a special use permit. In addition, a landscape plan, identifying vegetation that will be removed and planned revegetation efforts, must be submitted for approval. Substantial site grading, filling, terracing, and excavation is prohibited. Any other grading, filling, or excavation requires approval of final engineering plans and issuance of a special use permit by the village. Natural open channel drainage ways must be preserved.[11] Developers planning construction within wetlands or within 100 linear feet from the edge of designated wetlands must submit plans and reports to support approval of a special use permit.

The planning department is in the process of preparing amendments to the existing code in the areas of tree preservation, landscaping, weeds and nuisance species, existing tree protection, and the wetland overlay district. The changes would alter the existing wetland protection by broadening the defined wetland areas and moving from a wetlands overlay district to an ordinance that would protect wetlands as they are identified throughout the entire jurisdiction. To help delineate the new protected wetland areas, a consultant is conducting an inventory and prioritizing areas for protection. The department hopes that the amendments to its zoning ordinances will be adopted by the end of 2003. The proposed changes coincide with another department project to write a biodiversity recovery plan, which will become an amendment to the village's existing comprehensive plan.[12]

Stormwater Management/Sediment and Erosion Control

Description

Stormwater management ordinances are regulatory tools to control the impacts of stormwater runoff and discharge. Although these regulations may be found as stand-alone ordinances, they are frequently part of wetland protection, floodplain protection, and steep slopes ordinances. Stormwater management ordinances can include a range of features to minimize soil erosion, runoff of sediment and pollution, and flooding associated with the release of stormwater. For example, these ordinances can require tree and vegetation protection, the use of retention ponds to collect stormwater, the siting of roadways away from waterways, and design features such as the use of porous pavement or the design of curbs to facilitate concentration and collection of particulate matter. Stormwater management plans may also involve the creation of wetlands, since wetlands help control stormwater runoff by storing or regulating natural flows.[13]

Use for Biodiversity

Stormwater management is an essential function for many local governmental jurisdictions. Biodiversity-friendly approaches to stormwater emphasize the minimization of impervious surfaces and greater use of vegetated catch basins, swales, and infiltration areas. Stormwater ordinances that encourage the use of rain gardens, constructed wetlands, and similar "soft" infrastructure approaches have habitat benefits. Ordinances can also provide incentives or requirements for low impact development, which shrinks the amount of impervious surface for roads, driveways, parking lots, and other infrastructure. These techniques minimize the introduction of nutrients, chemicals, and pollutants to the environment, and also preserve some natural functions.

Key Biodiversity Elements

Stormwater management ordinances can support biodiversity conservation with consideration of several key elements:

1. The ordinance should specifically authorize the use of development designs and stormwater management systems that reduce impervious surfaces.

2. The ordinance should require developers to *consider* use of vegetation, wetlands, grass swales, buffers, and other "soft"structure management approaches as an alternative to concrete gutters and corporate ponds. The ordinance should allow the local government to approve these techniques throughout the jurisdiction. The ordinance should authorize the local government to require use of these techniques in specific instances and in specific areas identified in the comprehensive plan or zoning ordinance.

3. Ordinance drafters should consider establishing stormwater financing mechanisms that provide incentives to reduce impervious surfaces or use "soft" approaches. A stormwater management utility fee can be adopted with a sliding scale to encourage these choices.[14]

4. For publicly financed infrastructure, the ordinance and capital improvement plan should favor low impact development and soft infrastructure, including vegetation and infiltration methods.

Stormwater Control—Orlando, Florida

To address the effects of development on nearby lakes, the Public Works Department of Orlando, Florida, established an Urban Stormwater Management Program in the early 1980s. As part of this program, the city implemented a stormwater utility fee. Since 1989, the city's Stormwater Utility Bureau has used funds from the stormwater utility to protect and restore surface water bodies in the city. Some of these measures have habitat benefits.

The utility fee is based on the square footage of all residential and nonresidential parcels. Typical single-family residential lots of 7,760 square feet are required to pay a monthly fee of $5.50 ($66 per year). The maximum fee is $75.90 per year for single-family lots of 9,700 feet or larger and the minimum is $46.20 for single-family lots of 3,880 square feet and smaller. Properties with stormwater facilities are entitled to a reduced fee.[15] The revenues from the service fee are deposited in a stormwater fund and are used exclusively for Stormwater Utility Bureau purposes.[16] This utility funds a number of projects, including the operation, construction, and maintenance of stormwater management devices and the Urban Lake Enhancement Program, which addresses the city's 81 natural lakes and 23 water bodies created as borrow pits or stormwater ponds.

The Urban Lake Enhancement Program includes creation of wetlands, lake revegetation, lake aeration, pollution control devices, alum injection, street sweeping, drainage system maintenance, monitoring, and education. Through lake revegetation projects, the city planted 22 miles of shoreline in 45 lakes with native aquatic plants. The plants enable the lakes to assimilate nutrient inputs and provide increased wildlife habitat. Similarly, the city has created a number of wetland areas, including the Greenwood Urban Wetlands and the Lake Lorna Doone Wetlands.[17] The program also funds restoration activities. For example, Lake Lucerne is part of a natural lake system that receives stormwater runoff from 271 acres of high density commercial-industrial and residential developments constructed decades before modern stormwater controls. Orlando's Lake Enhancement Program uses a system to inject liquid alum, an acid salt that is used in lake restoration projects as a method of inactivating sediment release of phosphorous during anaerobic conditions, to restore some ecological function to the lake.

The city has monitored each lake since 1990 by collecting quarterly data from scientists and citizens participating in the LAKEWATCH program. The city assesses water quality by determining the trophic state of each lake, which is greatly affected by stormwater runoff. Regression analysis performed as part of a 2001 report on lake quality indicated that 13.3% of the lakes in the city have improving water quality trends and 8.4% have degrading trends, while the remaining 78.3% of the lakes did not have any significant changes over the past several years.[18]

Steep Slope Limitations

Description

Steep slope protection provisions limit building on steep slopes, mandate setbacks from wetlands and watercourses, and contain vegetative or other requirements to protect steep slopes from development impacts. They are often included in wetland and watercourse ordinances, as slopes affect the drainage of runoff into waterways. But they are also found as free-standing ordinances or associated with overlays intended to produce ridge lines or hilly habitat areas.

Use for Biodiversity

Steep slope ordinances are often addressed in part to safety concerns (defining buildable lots and portions of lots based on steepness of the grade), and in part to sediment and erosion control (as runoff is faster from steeper slopes and removal of vegetation can lead to greater impairment of water quality). In some areas, limitations are also intended to protect viewsheds and scenic resources. In addition to these common concerns, slopes provide distinct habitats and vegetation complexes owing to microclimates, differences in soils, and distinct disturbance regimes. Slope protection ordinances can integrate all of these concerns and help provide both key habitat areas and connections between habitats, as well as minimizing pollutant impacts.

Key Biodiversity Elements

Steep slope and mountain protection ordinances can protect biodiversity and ecological features with attention to the following key elements:

1. The ordinance should define the slopes comprised within the ordinance not only in terms of their hazard and steepness of the grade, but also designate them or provide for their designation based on natural heritage information.

2. The ordinance should explicitly limit the removal of vegetation, require the replacement of vegetation removed during construction, and include other means to protect water quality, vegetation, and habitat integrity. The ordinance may establish a preference for use of native species in restorations and revegetation of the slopes.

3. The ordinance should define suitable activities, densities, and development activities in order to minimize the creation of impervious surfaces and limit habitat fragmentation. Ordinance drafters may use density-limiting techniques and prescribe special infrastructure standards tailored to these areas.

4. Ordinance drafters should consider defining some steep slope areas as entirely off limits to construction if data support findings as to erosion, slope failure, water pollution, threat to downslope habitat areas and water bodies, or destruction of unique habitats (raptor habitats, escarpments, springs, and alpine bogs, for example).

Mountain Protection Plan—Pickens County, Georgia

Pickens County, in northern Georgia at the southern end of the Appalachian range, adopted a Mountain Protection Plan ordinance. The ordinance follows through on a state law that requires counties to prepare and implement comprehensive plan provisions that protect mountains based on state-adopted minimum criteria.[19] The state's criteria provide for mapping and for adoption of local conservation measures that address characteristics of the mountain area that "make it unique or significant in the conservation of flora and fauna including threatened, rare, and endangered species." County plans are required by the state's criteria to consider "the effect of activities within protected mountain areas on immediately adjacent sensitive natural areas."[20]

Pickens County adopted the ordinance to protect against increased erosion and stream sedimentation, landslides, groundwater contamination, habitat damage, and to protect the scenic and natural beauty of mountains vital to the local tourism economy.[21] The ordinance applies to any "protected mountain," defined as "all land area 2,200 feet or more above mean sea level, that has a percentage slope of 25[%] or greater for at least 500 feet horizontally," and includes the "crests, summits, and ridge tops" at elevations higher than any such area without regard to their slope. The ordinance also applies to land areas at 2,200 feet or more that have a slope of less than 25% but that are wholly within an otherwise protected mountain area, e.g., saddles and hollows.[22]

In these protected areas, state and county ordinances regulate hazardous waste disposal and handling, agriculture and forestry, mining, dwellings, and commercial structures. The county ordinance limits single-family dwellings to a density of not more than 1 per 10 acres (except for land previously subdivided and recorded) and multifamily dwellings to a gross density of not more than 1 dwelling unit per 10 acres.[23] This ordinance provision is more strict than the state standard limiting single-family dwellings to one per acre and multifamily dwellings to four dwelling units per acre, except under some conditions.[24] Commercial developments must submit a detailed landscaping plan identifying all the trees above eight inches in diameter that will be removed and a plan for the replacement of such trees. Plans for commercial developments also must include a topographical survey and an assessment of the effect of the construction and operation of the commercial property on the environment of the protected mountain.[25] In mountain protection areas no land-disturbing activity may remove more than 50% of trees exceeding eight inches in diameter without an approved reforestation plan. Structures with mountain protection areas may not exceed 40 feet in height.[26]

While Pickens County does not have a large amount of land over 2,200 feet, the ordinance reduces the likelihood of large-scale development on thousands of acres important to the county's wildlife habitat and natural and scenic areas.[27] The limitation on development helps minimize loss of ridgetops and mountain habitat areas and limits adverse effects on water quality by preventing a potential proliferation of dwelling units using septic systems in headwaters and slope areas unsuitable for such development.

NATURE-FRIENDLY ORDINANCES: LOCAL MEASURES TO CONSERVE BIODIVERSITY

Forest Conservation/Tree Protection

Description

Local governments can provide for the conservation of forests and tree cover in connection with development. Such provisions are designed to encourage developers to retain forest cover to the extent possible and to engage in reforestation to offset some of the losses associated with land-clearing and development activities. Various local jurisdictions across the country have tree conservation ordinances and provide for the retention and protection of trees in development areas. Maryland requires each unit of local government having planning and zoning authority to develop a forest conservation program with elements consistent with state law.[28] Comprehensive ordinances requiring tree retention and forest conservation in the context of development are not a taking of property rights.[29]

Use for Biodiversity

Forest conservation in development areas is important to maintain intact habitat patches and connectivity of forest areas. Forest retention and mitigation ordinances provide a way to ensure that biodiversity benefits are not sacrificed in connection with development.

Many communities undergoing rapid development experience substantial forest losses at the initial stage of the process. In many instances, developers find it easier to clear and grade the land in order to start with a clean slate for building than to tailor the development to the site characteristics. In addition, if the site contains any older, mature trees (particularly important for biodiversity and other values), sale of the timber in advance of development may help to provide cash flow during a time when there is little income to the developer. But the effects on biodiversity are both immediate and long-term. In the short term, forest habitat and diversity is lost, as is the water quality benefit of forest canopy. In the longer term, the attempt to recreate forest cover is a long-term project and usually fails to provide the structural diversity, the retention of natural processes, and the connectivity of retained forest patches. Communities, by ordinance, can address these concerns by requiring delineations of forests on development sites, by setting goals or requirements for forest retention or reforestation, by establishing requirements for connectivity of open space and forest areas on development sites, and by requiring suitable mitigation consistent with the purposes of the development. Benefits include not only biodiversity but water quality, community character, air quality, reduced utility expenses for residents of the development, active and passive recreation, and minimization of the cumulative effects of multiple land clearing activities going on within a few years and a few miles of one another.

Key Biodiversity Elements

Forest conservation ordinances can support biodiversity. They should have the following key elements:

1. The ordinance should define requirements for minimization of the amount of forest cover removed in connection with development. The ordinance should establish priorities for retention of undisturbed forest in particular areas that have value for biodiversity, including riparian areas, wetland areas, and areas connecting other forested habitats.

2. The ordinance should require submission of a forest delineation in connection with the submission of any subdivision or land development plan.

3. The ordinance should contain provisions that reach back for a period of years to prevent forest removal under the guise of timbering commercial logging that is really part of site preparation for development. This can be done through notice provisions or through the application of delineation and mitigation requirements to development applications that are filed within a certain number of years following a substantial removal of forest cover.

4. Forest cover and reforestation objectives should be spelled out explicitly by formula so that it is clear what should be retained or reforested.

5. The ordinance should provide for compensatory mitigation on-site where possible and in preferred areas such as off-site riparian areas where forest retention or reforestation cannot be fully accomplished on-site.

Forest Conservation—Carroll County, Maryland

Maryland's 1991 Forest Conservation Act requires each unit of local government having planning and zoning authority to develop a forest conservation program with elements consistent with the state law. The Act applies "to any public or private subdivision plan or application for a grading or sediment control permit on areas 40,000 square feet or greater."[30] The law does not apply to commercial logging and timber harvest operations, but does apply to such operations that are subject to a grading permit for development within five years after the logging or harvest operation (in order to prevent developers from escaping the requirement under the guise of commercial logging).

Under the law, developers must conduct a forest stand delineation and submit an acceptable forest conservation plan, which provides for forest retention and for reforestation meeting certain percentage goals.[31] The law also requires some afforestation of nonforested development areas in certain cases where existing forest cover is minimal.[32] For forest retention, the state law establishes priorities for which forested areas of the tract should be retained first to satisfy the numerical goals. These include sensitive areas, areas of contiguous forests that provide connectivity with other tracts, larger trees, and trees that are rare, threatened or endangered, or associated with historic structures. The law also establishes similar priorities for the location on the tract of planned reforestation and afforestation areas. These include riparian buffers, forest corridors, floodplains, and contiguous forests, all important areas for biodiversity.[33]

Developers must partially reforest areas that they deforest for the development. The reforestation requirement is linked to a "conservation threshold." The law defines the threshold based on the land use. The forest conservation threshold is set at 50% of the net tract area for development in agriculture and resource areas, 25% for medium density residential development, 20% for high density residential or institutional development, and 15% for commercial, industrial, mixed use, and planned unit developments.[34] For every acre cleared on the net tract area above the applicable forest conservation threshold, the tract must be reforested at a ratio of one-fourth acre planted for every acre removed. For every acre cleared below the threshold, the area of forest removed must be reforested at a ratio of two acres planted for every one acre removed. In addition, the state law and local ordinances credit against the total number of acres required to be reforested each acre of forest retained above the applicable forest conservation threshold. These requirements collectively reward forest retention by valuing it more than the reforestation of cleared areas.

Maryland requires that reforestation under the law must be accomplished within one or two growing seasons of completion of the project. If reforestation cannot be reasonably accomplished either on- or off-site, the developer must contribute money to a forest conservation fund that is used for off-site reforestation. Maryland counties must place forested or reforested land under conservation easement or other suitable long-term protection.

The state law allows local ordinances to be stricter and to set different thresholds. Carroll County is a formerly agricultural county that is undergoing rapid development as development pressures move northward and westward of Baltimore County. Carroll County's Forest Conservation Act requires that the reforestation ratio for any land development—other than that contained in agricultural districts—is one acre planted for every acre of forest removed.[35] In Carroll County, the developer must post a bond to assure performance of the forest conservation plan at $5,000 per acre to be reforested or afforested. Carroll County's priorities for the location of reforestation and afforestation include the following, in order of priority:

> [T]o establish or enhance forest buffers adjacent to streams; to establish or increase existing forested corridors to connect existing forests within and/or adjacent to the site to facilitate wildlife movement; to establish or enhance forest buffers adjacent to critical habitats where appropriate; to establish plantings to stabilize slopes of 25[%] or greater and slopes of 15[%] or greater...; to establish buffers between areas of different land uses where appropriate; and to establish forest areas adjacent to existing forests so as to increase the overall area of contiguous forest cover, where appropriate.[36]

Vegetation Controls

Description

Vegetation controls are special regulations controlling the types of vegetation planted in or removed from an area. Vegetation controls can promote and maintain native species and discourage the introduction and proliferation of invasive non-native plant species. A vegetation control ordinance could impose environmental design standards requiring developers to eradicate invasive species and plant native species. Or, as part of the subdivision review process, a locality could require eradication of invasive species and planting of native species. Regulations could also specify types of vegetation that must be maintained in designated greenways and wildlife corridors or require that a certain percentage of tree or vegetation cover remain on a site. A locality could also condition public funding on the adoption of vegetation controls by, for example, requiring the eradication of invasive species and the planting of native species for all municipal projects and infrastructure expenditures.

Some vegetation controls are adverse to native plants and biodiversity. For example, some municipal weed ordinances and lawn care nuisance ordinances lead to prohibitions on natural forms of vegetation. This, in turn, leads to overreliance by homeowners and corporate landowners on weed-killing pesticides and to widespread use of plant species that need to be mowed and that have little or no habitat value. Municipalities may want to review these ordinances to assure that they are accomplishing the community's desired objectives (usually aesthetic and to avoid harboring pest species such as the common Norway rat) without also leading to ill effects on the biological health of the local area, such as ordinances that unnecessarily prohibit prairie plants and warm season grasses, while favoring lawns, exotic ivies, and monocultures.

Use for Biodiversity

Vegetation ordinances can encourage or require the use of native and local species for public infrastructure and for development projects. They can also prohibit the introduction and spread of noxious invasive species (if state laws or home-rule authorities permit).[37] Such laws have slowed the introduction and spread of exotic species formerly used for erosion control, resulted in water conservation through xeriscaping requirements in arid communities, and provided habitat benefits through promoting local biodiversity. The resulting plant communities have had beneficial effects on insects, birds, mammals, and other parts of the biological community.

Key Biodiversity Elements

Ordinance drafters should keep the following key elements in mind when drafting a vegetation ordinance:

1. The ordinance should define the basis for vegetation regulation. The ordinance should link the requirements to habitat function, water conservation, ecosystem health, and avoidance of nuisance species.

2. Where vegetation protection ordinances are enacted, the ordinance should specify that existing native vegetation adequately protected by the developer will count toward the satisfaction of the applicable minimum landscaping requirements of the zoning code.

3. The ordinance should prohibit the introduction of invasive exotics by land developers during the development process.

4. The ordinance should provide for removal of state-listed invasive plants by landowners as authorized by state law, including procedures for securing abatement as a nuisance.

5. The ordinance should set a standard for public works and municipally owned lands so that native species are preferred or required in government supported projects and lands.

6. If the local governance has a weed ordinance or property maintenance standards ordinance, the standards should be reviewed with the state's natural heritage program to identify provisions that unnecessarily inhibit reasonable uses of native plants by landowners.

Vegetation Control—Clallam County, Washington

Washington State law since 1969 has required counties to have "noxious weed control boards." While the state legislation originally focused on agricultural weeds, in the 1980s, the definition of noxious weeds was extended to aggressive, non-native plants that threaten either the environment or the economy.[38] Washington's weed law makes landowners responsible for the eradication of Class A (state concern) and the control of Class B (county concern) noxious weeds on their property.[39] The law also allows for the definition of other weeds (Class C).[40]

The Clallam County Weed Board was established in 1997 after the State Weed Board determined that substantial occurrences of non-native plants were threatening the county's natural resources. The Clallam County Weed Board has five members who make policy decisions and hire and oversee the activities of a coordinator, who works hands-on to eradicate and control the spread of noxious weeds.[41] The Clallam County Weed Board has jurisdiction over all lands in Clallam and Jefferson counties, except federal and tribal lands. The board partners with the U.S. Forest Service with respect to federal forest lands.[42]

The county's weed program combats invasive weeds through detection, education, cooperation, and compliance activities. The board has the authority to inspect private lands for the presence of defined noxious weeds and notifies landowners when weeds are detected. The board also works to educate citizens through presentations, a newsletter, flyers, and consultations. In 2001, the weed program participated in 25 public presentations or events, responded to 358 requests for information, and provided 45 on-site consultations to identify plants or help owners with control. The Board also maintains a "noxious weed demonstration garden" for educational purposes, which shows not only the common noxious weeds, but also native plants that can be mistaken for them. The program works with public and private landowners and coalitions to deal with invasive exotic plants in two counties. The weed board notifies landowners of the presence of noxious weeds and monitors lands to ensure the proper treatment or eradication of the plants.

Washington State's noxious weed list identifies over 100 noxious weeds divided into three different classes with different control priorities. County weed lists must contain the two top-priority weed designates, but counties have flexibility to add weeds as appropriate to their area. Before assuming jurisdiction in Jefferson County, the Clallam County Weed Board had identified 23 species of noxious weeds mandated for control at 584 sites in Clallam County alone.[43] Currently, the number of sites with species mandated for control is estimated to be more than 700.

The board also administers specific projects that affect wildlife and conservation. The board is working with the Elwha Klallam Tribe and the Washington Conservation Corps to remove noxious weeds in the area before the Elwha dams are dismantled in Olympic National Park. In the Sequim Valley, the board is working with numerous state and local stakeholders to remove noxious weeds that are forcing Roosevelt elk from their habitat into other regions where they are involved in vehicle accidents and pose other nuisances. In the elk habitat, the Board is working to remove knapweed and the Ox Eye Daisy.[44]

Utility Right-of-Way Siting and Management

Description

Local governments are sometimes empowered to enact regulations and guidelines covering right-of-way siting and construction. Even where such authority is reserved to state laws, local governments may have some jurisdiction over utility siting in subdivisions and more limited authority on other lands. Local guidelines can seek to minimize damage to critical natural areas by siting the utility line in a proposed or existing roadway or using an existing right-of-way, or by requiring a minimum undisturbed buffer between the utility line and the natural area. Even where such regulation is reserved to state utility regulators, local governments can affect maintenance procedures or adopt regulations that are consistent with the state regulations. Voluntary efforts can also be taken by powerline and other right-of-way managers to reduce adverse effects.

Use for Biodiversity

Powerline corridors and other maintained linear rights-of-way can be barriers
to habitat quality. They can produce adverse effects through introduction of exotic species, loss of habitat, habitat fragmentation, and repeated disturbance.
But they can be managed to limit these effects. For example, vegetation on
rights-of-way can be "feathered" to avoid some edge effects, or the widths of
such rights-of-way can be reduced in order to minimize the migration barrier.[45]
Wildlife crossings can be constructed. Maintaining shrubby and low vegetative
cover can promote wildlife crossings and minimize undesirable corridor effects. *See* Figure 6. Judicious use of herbicides can also reduce the need for
large scale disturbance and redisturbance of the right-of-way and can also be
done on a schedule that assures that alternate sections are treated on different
schedules in order to provide habitat crossings and reservoirs of cover and food
even when maintenance is being performed.

Figure 6: Right-of-Way Management

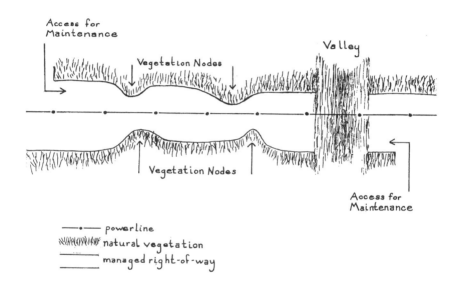

Drawing by Kathryn Hubler

NATURE-FRIENDLY ORDINANCES: LOCAL MEASURES TO CONSERVE BIODIVERSITY

Key Biodiversity Elements

Several elements are important for the protection of biodiversity:

1. The ordinance should, if feasible, specify priorities for the location and construction of rights-of-way that minimize habitat fragmentation and habitat disturbance.

2. The ordinance should specify management measures and standards for the maintenance of rights-of-way, including, where feasible, limitations on pesticide use, provision of areas for wildlife crossings, exclusion of exotic plant species, and scheduling of maintenance activities to avoid nesting and breeding seasons.

3. The ordinance drafter should consider whether to require notice to local government prior to right-of-way activities, in order to assure that compliance with the substantive requirements can be verified. Note that even if the local government has no authority to prescribe or regulate right-of-way maintenance activities, it may nevertheless adopt an ordinance requiring notice by the right-of-way owner to the local government prior to its conducting activities in order to allow the local government to request voluntary consultation with the utility. Such consultation can result in changes to timing of activities or alterations in activities to the benefit of the community and the environment.

Utility Siting and Management—Delmarva Peninsula

A company called Conectiv provides energy services in Delaware, Maryland, New Jersey, and Virginia. The company has a program to manage for habitat in utility rights-of-way and also coordinates with state agencies and the regional office of the U.S. Fish and Wildlife Service (FWS) to improve the habitat functionality of the land surrounding its powerlines. While some of these practices are voluntary and others address federal endangered species concerns, these approaches can be used in developing local ordinances, practices, and guidelines.

Traditionally, many power companies mow the vegetation surrounding powerlines every few years in order to remove tree species and broadly apply herbicides to kill tree sprouts and lower growing vegetation that may interfere with access or line management. Delmarva Power, which merged with Atlantic City Electric in 1998 to become Conectiv, started testing different uses of herbicides two decades ago to control maintenance costs and improve wildlife habitat. Tests indicated that controlled application of herbicides could allow low-growing plant and shrub species to flourish without detriment to right-of-way maintenance and at lower costs to the company.[46] Since that time, Conectiv has reduced the impact of its vegetation management practices to avoid adverse effects on plants that are not a threat to operations. In general, after the first mowing, subsequent vegetation treatments are carried out by workers who selectively apply herbicides to sprouts from root systems and seedlings of specified trees. Workers are trained to identify the species for removal and use maps created through a geographic information system to target the areas requiring treatment. The herbicide is chosen to target the plant to which it is applied.

The company has recognized a number of benefits from its selective vegetation management. The process of selecting trees for eradication and allowing low-growing plants to flourish has allowed diverse species to establish and maintain ecological integrity. These areas also provide habitat for meadow wildlife species that eat tree seeds and sprouts. Thus, the company's long-term maintenance costs are reduced to some extent by the self-sustaining wildlife habitat.[47] In addition, the low-growing plants that inhabit the area protect soils from erosion and buffer streams, protecting them from siltation. The herbicide treatments also provide more browse and cover for animal species than do areas that are periodically mowed.[48]

Conectiv also has a memorandum of understanding and works with the FWS to protect threatened and endangered species and habitat. The company has implemented measures to enhance utility rights-of-way to support the bog turtle—a threatened species in New Jersey that depends on open meadow. The turtle's habitat has deteriorated and disappeared due to development and to the effects of invasive species. Conectiv workers created meadow habitat by removing vegetation, specifically *Phragmites australis*, an invasive species particularly troublesome for the turtle. Similarly, the company restored a former forested wetland area to provide habitat for the swamp pink in an area that had previously been mechanically mowed. Conectiv treated only the trees in the designated areas, leaving medium and low-growth shrubs to provide the necessary shade for the federally listed threatened plant.

Conectiv also has memoranda of understanding (MOU) and informal agreements with the states. In Delaware and Maryland, the company has an agreement with the natural heritage programs to obtain maps of rare plants. The company has also worked with the natural heritage program in Delaware to encourage private landowners to allow bird census takers to walk on rights-of-way and count bird species. The Edison Electric Institute is working to develop a national MOU for federal agencies to use Conectiv's best management practice on utility rights-of-way.[49]

Chapter Seven Endnotes

1. An introduction to the literature of buffer areas is summarized in ENVIRONMENTAL LAW INSTITUTE, CONSERVATION THRESHOLDS FOR LAND USE PLANNERS (2003), *available at* http://www.elistore.org (last visited Dec. 11, 2003).

2. HOWARD COUNTY DEP'T OF PLANNING & ZONING, GENERAL PLAN (2000), *available at* http://www.co.ho.md.us/DPZ/GP2000/genplan2k.htm (last visited Jan. 5, 2004).

3. HOWARD COUNTY, MD., SUBDIVISION AND LAND DEVELOPMENT REGULATIONS (2002), *available at* http://www.co.ho.md.us/DPZ/DPZdocs/SubdivisionRegs Completebook100203.pdf (last visited Jan. 5, 2004).

4. *Id.*

5. *Id.*

6. HOWARD COUNTY DEP'T OF PLANNING & ZONING, *supra* note 2.

7. *Id.*

8. SCHAUMBURG, ILL., ORD. 163 (passed Dec. 12, 1961); SCHAUMBURG, ILL., AM. ORD. 95-62 (passed June 13, 1995).

9. VILLAGE OF SCHAUMBURG, ILL., CODE OF ORDINANCES tit. 15, ch. 154, §154.196(A) (2003) (Village of Schaumburg Wetland Protection Overlay District), *at* http://ordlink.com/codes/schaumbu/ (last visited Dec. 11, 2003).

10. *Id.* §154.196(A)1-7.

11. *Id.* §154.196(D)(4)-(5).

12. Telephone Interview with Phyllis Weller, Senior Planner, Village of Schaumburg (Mar. 20, 2003).

13. A useful guide to stormwater strategies with examples from hundreds of communities around the United States is NATURAL RESOURCES DEFENSE COUNCIL, INC., STORM-WATER STRATEGIES: COMMUNITY RESPONSES TO RUNOFF POLLUTION (1999).

14. *See* JAMES M. MCELFISH JR. & SUSAN CASEY-LEFKOWITZ, SMART GROWTH AND THE CLEAN WATER ACT 23-30 (Northeast-Midwest Institute 2001), *available at* http://www.nemw.org (last visited Dec. 11, 2003).

15. City of Orlando Stormwater Utility, *Frequently Asked Questions*, *at* http://www.cityoforlando.net/public_works/stormwater/faq.htm (last visited Mar. 4, 2003).

16. ORLANDO, FLA., CITY CODE §31.14 (Oct. 1995, as amended Oct. 1996).

17. STORMWATER UTILITY BUREAU, PUBLIC WORKS DEP'T, CITY OF ORLANDO STORM-WATER UTILITY, ENVIRONMENTAL FUNCTIONS (2000).

18. CITY OF ORLANDO, 2001 LAKE WATER QUALITY REPORT (2002), *available at* http://www.cityoforlando.net/public_works/stormwater/wqr01/index.htm (last visited Dec. 11, 2003).

19. GA. CODE ANN. §12-28-8(b), (h).

20. GA. R. & REGS., CRITERIA FOR MOUNTAIN PROTECTION §391-3-.16-.05, *available at* http://www.state.ga.us/rules/index.cgi?base=391/3/16/16 (last visited Jan. 7, 2004).

21. CODE OF ORDINANCES OF PICKENS COUNTY, GA. 26.92.

22. *Id.* 26.93.

23. *Id.* 26.96(4).

24. GA. CODE ANN. §12-2-8(h).

25. CODE OF ORDINANCES OF PICKENS COUNTY, GA. 26.96(6).

26. *Id.* 26.97.

27. Telephone Interview with Rodney Buckingham, Pickens County (Feb. 19, 2003).

28. MD. CODE ANN., NAT. RES. §§5-1601 et seq.

29. Greater Atlanta Homebuilders Ass'n v. DeKalb County, 588 S.E.2d 694 (Ga. 2003).

30. MD. CODE ANN., NAT. RES. §5-1602.

31. The planning process is described in Michael F. Galvin et al., *Maryland's Forest Con-servation Act: A Process for Urban Greenspace Protection During the Development Process*, 26 J. ARBORICULTURE 275-80 (Sept. 2000), *available at* http://dnrweb.dnr.state.md.us/download/forests/fca.pdf (last visited Dec. 11, 2003).

32. MD. CODE ANN., NAT. RES. §5-1606.

33. *Id.* §5-1607.

34. *Id.* §5-1606.

35. CARROLL COUNTY, MD., CODE ch. 115, §115-8 (Forest Conservation).

36. *Id.* §115-10.

37. For more information on state laws and programs affecting control of invasive exotic species, see MEG FILBEY ET AL., HALTING THE INVASION (Envtl. L. Inst. 2002), *available at* http://www.elistore.org/reports_detail.asp?ID=10678 (last visited Dec. 11, 2003).

38. Clallam County, Washington, *Noxious Weed Control Homepage*, *at* http://www.clallam.net/weedcontrol/ (last visited Dec. 11, 2003).

39. *Id.*

40. WASH. REV. CODE §17.10 (Noxious Weeds—Control Boards).

41. Clallam County, *supra* note 38.

42. Telephone Interviews with Clallam County Weed Board Coordinator (Sept. 13-16, 2002) [hereinafter Clallam County Weed Board Coordinator Interviews].

43. Clallam County, *supra* note 38.

44. Clallam County Weed Board Coordinator Interviews, *supra* note 42.

45. J. Edward Gates, *Powerline Corridors, Edge Effects, and Wildlife in Forested Land-scapes of the Central Appalachians, in* WILDLIFE AND HABITAT IN MANAGED LAND-SCAPES (J.E. Rodiek & E.G. Bolen eds., Island Press 1991).

46. Richard A. Johnstone, *Vegetation Management: Mowing to Spraying*, 16 J. ARBORI-CULTURE 186 (July 1990).

47. Telephone Interview with Richard Johnstone, Conectiv (Jan. 15, 2003) [hereinafter Johnstone Interview].

48. Johnstone, *supra* note 46.

49. Johnstone Interview, *supra* note 47.

Chapter Eight—Public Open Space Acquisition and Management

L ocal governments acquire and own lands and waters for a variety of purposes. Many local government and school district acquisition programs can be structured to include some recognition of biodiversity values, and publicly owned lands can be managed for multiple purposes including biodiversity conservation. Local governments can establish criteria and management objectives for their land ownership and management programs.

The acquisition and management of open space lands should rely on good planning and can take advantage of land conservation and planning tools that are designed to support the value and well-being of communities in general.[1] This chapter covers:

- Purchase of Open Space or Conservation Easements[2];
- Public Open Space Management; and
- Urban Retrofitting.

Purchase of Open Space or Conservation Easements

Description

Local governments often engage in land acquisition for purposes of conservation, recreation, watershed protection, and farmland protection. Most state-enabling laws and home-rule charters provide sufficient authority for local governments to engage in programs of this sort, using their own bonding authority, general revenues, specifically designated tax increments, or grants from state and federal open space, park, and farmland preservation programs.[3]

Many conservation acquisition programs now recognize the value of conservation easements (also called conservation restrictions in some parts of the country) whereby the development interest in the property is conveyed to a governmental entity or conservation-oriented nonprofit organization while the landowner retains fee title to the property and the ability to engage in residual uses consistent with the easement.

Various types of acquisition programs exist including ones that provide for outright purchase or donation purchase of the interests from willing sellers, to installment purchase arrangements such as those used in some Maryland counties where the county buys development rights with a long-term promissory note; the landowner gets semiannual payments, with a balloon payment due in the future, while the county finances the acquisition with purchase of long-term treasury bonds. A similar approach is used in the Virginia Beach Purchase of Development Rights program described in Chapter Six.

NATURE-FRIENDLY ORDINANCES: LOCAL MEASURES TO CONSERVE BIODIVERSITY

Use for Biodiversity

Land acquisition can be an important tool for biodiversity, but unless biological diversity conservation is part of the local government's program, biodiversity is not necessarily conserved by open space purchases. Conversion of open space sites to some forms of intensive recreation may be incompatible with some biodiversity objectives. Similarly, a riparian greenway can lose some of its ecological integrity if the local government constructs a paved bikeway along its length without attention to buffer zones, wildlife crossings, maintenance of diverse vegetation and stream shading, and stream bank protection. Planning open space acquisitions to serve multiple objectives and careful attention to parcel size, fragmentation, habitat connections, and natural disturbance patterns can make acquisition a powerful tool for local governments.

Key Biodiversity Elements

Biodiversity can be integrated into land acquisition in two ways:

1. The local government should include biodiversity as an explicit goal of its land acquisition program.

2. The local government should assure that biodiversity values are represented in acquisitions conducted to serve another primary purpose by including these values in the plan for other acquisition programs.

Acquisition of Open Space and Conservation Easements—Fall River and Worcester, Massachusetts

State and local funding can be used to target land acquisitions to serve multiple uses for municipalities. Several Massachusetts cities have made good use of biodiversity information to identify and protect areas of significant biological value.

The city of Fall River's western 12 square miles are densely developed, while the eastern 12 square miles are undeveloped and include the city's drinking water reservoirs and thousands of acres of forestland. With help from the commonwealth's Department of Environmental Management (DEM), the Department of Fisheries, Wildlife, and Environmental Law Enforcement (DFWELE), and The Trustees of Reservations, the city of Fall River assured the protection of 13,600 acres that officially became the state's first recognized "Bioreserve" in October 2002. The city purchased 3,800 privately owned acres to help meet its goal for quality of life and long-term protection of open space. In connection with the acquisition, the city granted a conservation restriction to the commonwealth on the adjacent 4,300-acre city water supply lands to ensure that these lands will also be permanently protected from development. These two holdings, together with the adjacent 5,100-acre Freetown-Fall River State Forest, make up a permanently protected area that will be jointly managed by the DEM, the DFWELE, Fall River, and the Trustees of Reservations as the state's first Bioreserve, a conservation area large enough to protect native plant and animal species representative of southeastern Massachusetts, while also making land available for recreation, nature trails, and daily educational programs. The total acquisition costs were $9.6 million for land and conservation restrictions.[4]

The city of Worcester's conservation commission worked closely with staff at the Massachusetts Audubon Society on an acquisition of 103 acres of undeveloped land adjacent to the Society's Broad Meadow Brook Sanctuary in 2001. The Massachusetts Natural Heritage and Endangered Species program had identified this property as a state significant natural heritage resource and it was listed as a high priority in the city's own "What's Left" report identifying undeveloped parcels still remaining in Worcester. The oak savannah found on this property, characterized by low grasses and blueberries, provides necessary habitat for migratory birds and butterflies, as well as the native New England birds and animals generally found in more rural areas. This project was also a unique opportunity to add to a "greenway hub" in the state's second largest city. This urban conservation acquisition enlarged an existing 270-acre block of legally protected open space, creating the largest urban sanctuary in New England.[5] The city purchased the property from Catholic Charities for $700,000, including a $250,000 grant from the commonwealth's Division of Conservation Services and an additional $156,000 from the federal Land and Water Conservation Fund Program to help pay for the purchase.

Public Open Space Management

Description

Local governments own a great deal of land, including land used for open space and recreation, land used for schools and government facilities, watershed lands, maintenance facilities, and other lands. Many of these lands are managed according to local standard operating procedures, and many are managed only for the single purpose for which they are held.

Adoption of conservation management ordinances and procedures offers an opportunity to integrate biodiversity conservation into the day-to-day management of lands and into the strategic planning for how lands will be held and used. Such standards can include provisions to exclude invasive exotic species; procedures for tree retention, maintenance, and replacement; and procedures for ecological restoration and maintenance activities, among others.

Use for Biodiversity

Many publicly owned lands offer substantial opportunities for biodiversity conservation, especially for restoration activities. Without an explicit management plan or guidance from municipal ordinances, however, many of these opportunities will be missed. Nearly all of the conservation guidelines can be met on publicly owned lands, including parklands and school lands.

Some of the management approaches can include requirements to leave seed trees and some standing dead trees (to mimic natural processes), to provide for recovery of riverbanks, to manage parks to provide for fallow and no-mow areas, and preparation of specific plans for restoration of lands and removal of exotic species.

Key Biodiversity Elements .

Management of publicly owned lands can serve biodiversity objectives if the local government pays attention to several key elements:

1. The local government should adopt a written management program for its publicly owned lands that includes biodiversity as a specific objective and that specifies a set of management measures.

2. The plan should provide a process for review of construction and siting of facilities to ensure their compatibility with biodiversity.

3. The plan should identify specific restoration plans and goals for the lands covered by the plan.

Public Open Space Management—St. Charles Township, Kane County, Illinois

St. Charles Park District in Kane County, Illinois, manages several natural open space areas for biodiversity as well as for recreation. The Park District is the public agency charged with providing public park and recreational services to the residents of St. Charles Township. In response to public interest in the existing natural areas and citizen concern over fragmented landscapes and the influx of aggressive, non-native weeds, in 1991 the Park District implemented a policy to acquire and manage lands to protect and restore natural areas and to provide environmental education. At the time, the district owned three natural areas and was leasing a fourth. Today the district manages 10 natural areas in addition to its developed recreational facility park lands. Two of these 10 are designated "nature preserves" where very little direct human activity or park development is authorized.[6]

Park District planning efforts made it possible to set in motion an effective acquisition and management program for areas with ecological and biodiversity significance. These included a 1988 Park and Recreation Study followed by a 1990 Comprehensive Parks and Recreation Master Plan. These were further informed by inventories of available open space in the township conducted in 1989 and 1992.

In 1996, the Park District finalized a new Comprehensive Master Plan for its lands. The plan includes both a specific land acquisition strategy and management goals for the lands. The plan calls for acquisition and preservation of open space and high quality natural areas—land that "can protect wildlife and fragile ecosystems and provide for a variety of recreational uses." In addition, the pro-

gram seeks acquisitions, such as greenways, that can "link open space areas."
The plan calls for the district to cooperate with other public and private entities
in the acquisition and development of open space to address both "recreation
needs and the preservation of significant environmental areas."[7]

Decisions on which lands to acquire under the strategy are based on a number
of factors, including ecological systems represented and the lands' availability.
Some parcels are acquired through open space requirements for development.
These exactions result in donations of land or payments of money per acre of
developed area. Mitigation programs, such as wetland mitigation banks, also
add to the inventory and provide funding for restoration activities. Other lands
are donated by The Nature Conservancy or private citizens.[8] But acquisition is
only part of the program.

What is especially interesting about the Park District's approach to management of its natural area lands is the attention given to wildlife and ecological processes. The 10 "natural areas" administered by the Park District include 2 nature
preserves and 8 park and wetland areas. The largest natural area is 340 acres
while the smallest is a 3-acre wetland park. The natural area lands managed by
the district total approximately 580 acres, out of a total parkland base of 1,100
acres managed by the district. (Another 1,100 acres of parkland are managed by
other public entities including the Kane County Forest Preserve District.)[9] Thus,
areas dedicated to natural communities and to ecological management measures
reflect a substantial percentage of the public parkland in this township.

The Park District has an adopted management plan for the natural areas and
maintains detailed records of activities at each area. The goals include managing the natural areas to maintain their native plant and animal communities, to
provide for passive recreation, and to offer interpretation and education to the
community. Objectives are set out for the areas. For example, in the Campton
Hills Park, the largest of the natural areas, the management plan identifies the
primary management objective as "to preserve and restore [the park] as an example of the presettlement landscape of Illinois and to provide habitat for native plants and animals of Illinois including several rare species."[10] In Campton
Hills, the Park District has removed thousands of cubic yards of fill and junk
from a wetland and continues to remove exotic plants and to plant native species in order to fulfill the objectives of the management plan. The hydrologic
restoration of this site has enabled wetland species to return.

Restoration activities are a substantial part of the management measures
used in the natural areas, as the lands include areas where wetland hydrology
has been altered and where invasive exotic species are a continuing threat. Ongoing activities include restoration of hydrology, the spraying and burning of
invasive species, cutting back aggressive grasses, planting native seeds, and, in
some of the natural areas, restoring fire to landscape processes. In the Otter
Creek Bend Wetland, the Park District restored a former cornfield to a functioning wetland ecosystem. Workers restored the hydrological system by breaking
the agricultural drain tiles and making low, ponded areas in old floodway
swales. Workers then planted the site with wetland plant species and built a
trail, a bridge, and an overlook. A contractor applied herbicides to invasive

plants, burned the vegetation on the site, mowed weeds, and set up monitoring transects until the district assumed management of the area.[11]

The district's two nature preserves, Ferson Creek Fen and Norris Woods, are very high quality natural areas with written management plans where public projects and off-trail activity are prohibited.

Urban Retrofitting

Description

In areas that have long been developed, open space lands may be scarce. In such areas, local governments may target acquisition programs toward parcels that have an existing use but that can be retrofitted for park, recreation, open space, and biodiversity uses. If the local government has established criteria for such acquisitions and a funding mechanism, properties can be acquired and assemble from willing sellers, estates, or even assembled from tax delinquent or vacant properties.

Use for Biodiversity

Parcels of land that have been previously developed but that provide key connections between open space parcels or that contain unique natural features can be protected and conserved by a program that has identified such parcels for future acquisition. For example, consider an older urban municipality with a declining tax base and pockets of tax delinquent vacant properties. In some instances these properties may be located in areas along urban stream corridors or adjacent to public school and municipal parklands. If the municipality has evaluated the opportunities for conservation even though it is essentially land-locked and fully developed, it can target its acquisition of these properties and assemble them to serve conservation goals. Sources of funding may include community development block grants, state open space and recreation funding, private donations and foundation funding, or tax or bond funds. More affluent municipalities may be able to develop focused programs to identify and acquire such lands using their own tax and bond funding. While urban retrofitting is not typically able to conserve large parcels or to restore large habitat areas, it can serve the biodiversity goals of conserving unique and sensitive areas and providing connections between other habitat areas.

Key Elements for Biodiversity

A local government can identify retrofitting opportunities for urban conservation with attention to the following key elements:

1. Establish a planning and inventory process that can identify privately owned lands that have potential characteristics that can support conservation. At a minimum, establish criteria that identify the values of open space lands that may be suitable for acquisition at some time in

the future (even if specific areas or parcels are not identified).

2. Emphasize unique natural features and contiguousness or connectivity with other open space areas as key criteria for acquisition
and restoration.

3. For acquired properties, adopt programs and policies that maintain
the natural characteristics that make the lands suitable for conservation acquisition.

Urban Retrofitting—Arlington, Virginia

Arlington is an affluent, densely populated county across the Potomac River
from Washington, D.C. It has substantial residential and commercial development and has been essentially "built out" for several decades. Current development activities are largely focused on residential infill development (placing
more homes on previously developed parcels after demolishing the older housing), and mixed use and commercial development, including offices and
densely developed "urban village" commercial centers replacing single-story
commercial buildings.

Because Arlington has been entirely subdivided and developed, opportunities for the assembly of additional open space for public recreation and conservation are limited. Nevertheless, the county board has established a long-term
plan for recreation and conservation lands, supplementing the 1,145 acres of
parkland and greenways managed by the county prior to the development of the
most recent plan in 1994. In its 1994 Open Space Master Plan, Arlington established a goal of assuring "for this and future generations the provision of an adequate supply of beneficial open space which is safe, accessible, and enjoy-
able."[12] Under this goal, the county adopted a number of objectives including:
"[P]aying particular attention to the protection of important threatened natural,
cultural[,] and historic resources," the acquisition of open space in "neighbor-
hood/residential areas to provide an attractive and healthful environment," and
preserving "appropriate areas to conserve ecological resources, protect streams
and environmentally significant areas" and historic resources.[13] The county
also set goals for acquisition of additional acreage of parkland and identified in
general terms areas where such land could be valuable.

Based on this planning process, in 1997 the county acquired three single-
family homes fronting on a busy urban street in a part of the county where developers were acquiring older homes in order to tear them down and erect larger
numbers of infill homes. These homes, originally constructed in the 1950s,
were on 1.5- to 2.5-acre lots (in a part of the county where one-quarter-acre or
smaller lots are now more typical). The importance of the acquisition was that
these lots, although fronting on a busy boulevard, were fairly deep and in their
rear areas contained the headwaters of a spring. The parcels also lay between a
regional park (Upton Hills), and a private swim club and public school, thus
providing a potential linear connection (at least a habitat connection) among
these public and privately owned parcels. The 5.34-acre parcel (assembled

from the three single-family home parcels) was then subject to a public planning process resulting in the decision to use the half of the land nearest the boulevard for a developed public skate park and youth-sized soccer field, and the rearward half of the land as a nature area and buffer zone for the spring, with a transitional "children's rain garden" demonstration area in between. The 1999 plan was approved, and funding for the park's development and other activities (including demolition of the three houses) was approved as part of a 2000 countywide park bond referendum.

Construction activities on Powhatan Springs Park began in 2003. The resulting recreation land will serve the recreational needs of county residents, while the conservation half of the parcel provides public protection and management of an important feature (the headwaters of an urban stream) and connectivity of habitat among public and private lands. A biological survey of the park discovered flourishing communities of salamanders and other amphibians, and the potential for ecological restoration (via removal of exotic invasive plants from the vicinity of the spring) is part of the longer term vision for management of the area.

Chapter Eight Endnotes

1. *See* TRUST FOR PUBLIC LAND & NATIONAL ASS'N OF COUNTIES, LOCAL
   GREENPRINTING FOR GROWTH: USING LAND CONSERVATION TO GUIDE GROWTH
   AND PRESERVE THE CHARACTERS OF OUR COMMUNITIES (2002), *available at*
   http://www.tpl.org and http://www.naco.org (last visited Dec. 12, 2003).

2. Purchase of Development Rights, covered in Chapter Six, is another purchase technique that also can result in permanent protection of open space, with potential
   biodiversity benefits if it is targeted toward lands with biodiversity values.

3. JOHN NOLON, OPEN GROUND: EFFECTIVE LOCAL STRATEGIES FOR PROTECTING NAT-
   URAL RESOURCES 519-42 (Envtl. L. Inst. 2003).

4. Press Release, Fall River, Massachusetts, Southeastern Massachusetts Bioreserve:
   Forest Will Become Parkland in Bioreserve, *at* http://www.fallriverma.org/press
   articles.asp?ID=7 (last visited Jan. 5, 2004).

5. *See* JAMES M. MCELFISH JR., SMART LINKS: TURNING CONSERVATION DOLLARS
   INTO SMART GROWTH OPPORTUNITIES 12 (Envtl. L. Inst. 2002), *available at* http://
   www.elistore.org/reports_detail.asp?ID=10665 (last visited Dec. 11, 2003).

6. St. Charles Park District website, *at* http://www.st-charlesparks.org/ (last visited Dec.
   12, 2003).

7. St. Charles Park District, *Master Plan Highlights, at* http://www.st-charlesparks.org/
   links/masterplanhighlights.htm (last visited Dec. 12, 2003).

8. Telephone Interview with Mary Ochsenschlager, Manager of Natural Resources and
   Interpretive Services, St. Charles Park District (Aug. 14, 2002).

9. St. Charles Park District website, *supra* note 7.

10. ST. CHARLES PARK DISTRICT, SITE ASSESSMENT AND MANAGEMENT RECOMMENDA-
    TIONS FOR CAMPTON HILLS PARK pt. II (Management Plan) (1991).

11. Telephone Interview with Mary Ochsenschlager, Manager of Natural Resources and
    Interpretive Services, St. Charles Park District (Sept. 17, 2002).

12. ARLINGTON COUNTY, OPEN SPACE MASTER PLAN (1994), *available at* http://www.
    co.arlington.va.us/prcr/scripts/planning/osmp.pdf (last visited Dec. 12, 2003).

13. *Id.*

Chapter Nine—Conclusion

Local governments are in the biodiversity business whether they recognize it or not. Currently, few do. But the familiar planning and land use development tools that help communities address other aspects of land use and the general welfare of the community are no less useful in ensuring the function of the living environment around us.

Over the last three decades, ecologists and conservation biologists have advanced our scientific understanding of living organisms and their life requirements by substantial amounts. Now, they are seeking to communicate these new understandings to the community of land use planners and decision-makers. The whole discipline of conservation biology is an attempt to connect scientific understanding to real-world decisions on the landscape. And the work of the Ecological Society of America's Land Use Committee represents a similar effort by the nation's ecologists.

At the same time, graduates of the nation's schools of planning and landscape architecture and a new generation of citizen activists and elected officials are realizing the critical importance of scientific knowledge to the long-term well-being of their communities. Whether or not they think in biodiversity terms, they recognize that a "nature-friendly" ordinance is generally to be preferred over one that is not. They are seeking to expand their knowledge of conservation, but do so by seeking practical advice and direction.

In short, each set of disciplines has begun to grow toward the other. While no single approach to integration of biodiversity into land use ordinances has caught on around the nation, hundreds of counties and municipalities are recognizing that they can do something positive to ensure that the landscape continues to support plants, animals, insects, fish, reptiles, birds, amphibians, and many other forms of life that make their communities special.

It is clearly a difficulty that the geographic scale of ecosystems and biological communities is generally much wider than the jurisdiction of planning boards and town councils. But states and conservation organizations are beginning to fill that knowledge gap.

It is really up to local governments to seek out sources of good information and to apply those overarching principles identified in Chapter Two: "Examine impacts of local decisions in a regional context," and "examine impacts of local decisions over time, considering foreseeable changes in the landscape." Then the available data can be integrated into comprehensive plans, zoning ordinances, subdivision ordinances, and a host of specific environmental and infrastructure controls and capital improvement plans.

This book has had little to say about integration of the land use tools it separately describes. But it should be apparent that almost every tool is connected in some way with several others. Boise's foothills plan involves subdivision controls and planned unit development. Baltimore County's urban services boundary is the same one as its comprehensive plan and zoning map dictate for rural and urban land uses. Milford Township's zoning performance standards are implemented in its subdivision and development review ordinance. Schaumburg's wetlands ordinance is tied to an overlay zone. Zoning in the Pine Barrens supports the transfer of development rights program. At their best, all of these land use tools carry out a coherent vision articulated in the comprehensive plan. But even in the absence of a comprehensive plan revision, almost every land use tool can be made more sensitive to biodiversity. If the needs of the biota are understood, then the land use tools can be marshaled to address those needs.

Recognizing that decades of unintended losses and mistakes should not be repeated, and drawing on the recognition that ecological science has come of age and has useful lessons to convey, citizens and local officials are expanding the scope of their concerns. Nature-friendly ordinances are the future of land use.